THE PENTATONIC PRESS INTEGRATED LEARNING SERIES
Teaching The Whole Child Through Music: Creative Play

From Wibbleton

to Wobbleton

Adventures with the elements of music and movement

JAMES HARDING

Illustrated by Eli Noyes

PENTATONIC
PRESS

A SPECIAL THANKS

If a picture is worth a hundred words, I would need to write a million of them to thank my illustrator, Eli Noyes, for his invaluable contribution to this book. Besides being an award-winning animator and graphic designer, Eli is a former San Francisco School parent as well as a musician himself. Working with him has been a true collaboration, where ideas inspired images and images inspired more ideas. If we had known how many illustrations would result we might not have had the nerve to start out in the first place! Seeing his delightful drawings populate Wibbleton has been one of my favorite parts of this journey.

Printed in the U.S.A. No part of this publication may be reproduced, stored in a retrieval system or transmitted, in any form, by any means, electronic, mechanical, photocopying, recording or otherwise, without the prior written permission of the publisher: Pentatonic Press, 1232 Second Avenue, San Francisco, CA 94122

For further information, go to: www.pentatonicpress.com

Illustrations and cover design: Eli Noyes
Editor: Peter Greenwood
Copy Editor: Corrine Olague
Book design and typesetting: Bill Holab Music

ISBN-10: 0977371255
ISBN-13: 978-0977371259

Second Printing

TABLE OF CONTENTS

FOREWORD

by Sofía López-Ibor[*]

It's no accident that the title of this book, "From Wibbleton to Wobbleton," refers to a pathway, a journey from a point of departure to a destination. The pedagogical philosophy of Orff Schulwerk places great value upon the pleasure of voyaging together with the students in an educational process that is full of moments of shared discovery.

James Harding, in his own unmistakable style, presents in these pages a wealth of examples and variations of how to invite students on the journey of making music. Each of these small adventures unfolds within an enticing world of aesthetic pleasure and sensory stimulus. The care with which James selects his didactic materials and the intelligent development of the activities for the class are hallmarks of his particular gift as a teacher.

In James' compass, true north is the child. It's evident from these lessons that he is well acquainted with the child's world. In his many years as a teacher he has observed what children like, their interests, how they play and how they learn, not to mention their sense of humor!

Like all good travel books, *From Wibbleton to Wobbleton* has an adventurous and exploratory spirit. Flipping through its pages you can see that the exploration of materials and teaching objects happens by means of a modus operandi which delights in variety, but which at the same time moves in a clear, logical sequence. The musical materials which James puts forth are chosen to develop not only the musicianship of the students but also their general aesthetic sense and their love for music.

This book is an ideal manual for all those who dare to take the adventure of making music with students of diverse ages. The hands-on and playful activities described in these pages will delight both you and your students. In our almost twenty years of collaboration, teaching children and teachers all around the world, I have witnessed first hand that James Harding is uniquely capable of surprising all of us with his ingenuity and his artful teaching.

---

[*] Sofia López-Ibor teaches at The San Francisco School. She is the author of *¡Quien canta su mal espanta!* (Schott 2004) and *Blue is the Sea* (Pentatonic Press 2011).

INTRODUCTION

From where to where?
I hope you didn't buy this book in a travel book store! Reading this book will not get you to Wobbleton, or to Wibbleton, for that matter. The journeys mapped out in the pages that follow will begin and end in the classroom. The travelers will be you and your students. The terrain that you will cross will be made of ideas, and your vehicles will be music and movement, rhyme, poetry, proverb, drama, science, math and visual art.

Adventures at school
If education is a journey, too often it feels to children like a forced march! As teachers, we need to pay attention to what makes learning come alive for our students. Anticipation, surprise, time to explore, and a sense of possibility make for a true adventure. Throw in a pinch of risk and most importantly, lots of play, and you have the kind of experience that will make music class one of their favorite times of the school day.

*Play is our brain's favorite way of learning.**

—Diane Ackerman
Author of *A Natural History of the Senses*

Child's play is serious business! We all know the feeling of "flow" which comes in true play- a sense of purpose and freedom at the same time which is absolutely delicious. Science has shown us that the mind registers emotional states along with any other information that it is receiving, and so any discoveries that are made in a state of play are likely to be pleasant and long-lasting ones.

A child loves her play
Not because it is easy
But because it is hard.†

—Dr. Benjamin Spock
Pediatrician and Author

Play and challenge
Kids hunger for challenge, and part of our job as teachers is to keep serving up appetizing problems for them to solve. A class, when it's humming along, is like a kite in the air with a steady breeze. Challenge is like the tension in the string: the more we pull, the higher the kite soars. But if we pull suddenly or too hard, the line snaps- discouragement! If we give no resistance, the kite flutters limply to the ground- boredom! All of the lessons in this book contain games and

---

* Diane Ackerman, *Deep Play* (New York: Vintage, 2000), 15
† Dr. Benjamin Spock. *Baby and Child Care* (New York: Pocket Books, Inc., 1961), 304

exercises for keeping your students on their toes. You will need to modify the level of challenge to meet the needs of your class. With luck, you'll enjoy one of my favorite sights as a teacher: eyes flashing with happy defiance, saying "Watch this! I can do it!"

Playful tone

Making music together is a wonderful test of our attention; the more attention we pay, the better the music sounds. A playful tone in the class inspires students to try their best and even to enjoy their mistakes.

An example of a musical attention challenge for young children is hearing the hidden rests at the ends of phrases:

"Clap when you hear a silent space in the poem…"

"Billy and me."…clap
"One two three"…clap
"I like coffee **and** Billy likes tea!"…. clap

On the last line, many children will anticipate the pattern set up by the first two lines and clap mistakenly on the word "and." As a teacher, I am hoping that someone will make this mistake and laugh, realizing that there's something tricky here. I can then say "Gotcha!" and challenge her to listen even more carefully for the pattern of long and short phrases. If my tone is light, she'll be eager to try again and get it right.

Play on the way

In a workshop with Wolfgang Hartmann* I was struck by an image he used: the "creative landing." He explained that many times as music teachers we are hoping to get our students to "climb the stairs" toward a particular goal—mastering a piece of music or dance, for instance. Yet even with such a goal there is always room to stop for a while to play creatively with some of the elements of the material we are teaching. This he called the "creative landing" on the staircase. Sometimes in the process of arriving at a particular goal we can have more than one landing. Another way I have of describing this is "play on the way." And, of course, the result of this play can range from a fun diversion to an exercise that contributes to a unique performance of the material in question. Either way the students' connection with the material is always strengthened by such play.

HOW TO USE THIS BOOK

Classroom teachers

If you are looking for a way to teach music in your classes, hooray! This book will give you ideas and activities for entering music with children. Don't have instruments? Many of these materials can be explored with just the voice, body and imagination.

If you are looking to use music to enhance the teaching of other subjects in the classroom, bravo! Approaching concepts through music and movement can add a wonderful new dimension to your classes. Solve a math problem to the beat! Sing a map! Act out a tooth tradition from another culture! Dance the orbits of the planets! Perform an opera of school rules! As a music

---

* Wolfgang Hartmann lives in Spain and teaches Off Schulwerk workshops internationally and often at the Orff Institute in Salzburg.

specialist, I enjoy collaborating with my classroom teacher colleagues, and many of these lessons were inspired by the themes they were exploring with the children in their classes.

Music specialists

If you are already familiar with Orff Schulwerk, you will know what to do with these lessons. Take what you like, vary the sequence, adapt the arrangements to your own needs. Apply some of the ideas in these examples to your own repertoire of rhymes, songs and games.

If you are new to the Orff approach, I hope this book will intrigue you and make you want to know more. I have included an appendix called "What is Orff Schulwerk?" with a bibliography and list of resources for further training. I have also included an appendix "Playing with the Elements of Music" which attempts to identify the kinds of creative activities that are hallmarks of this elemental music pedagogy.

More than one way to travel

In most of these lessons I have suggested a sequence of activities leading from exploration to performance. You as the teacher will need to figure out how far (and how fast) your students will travel down any of these roads. You might use some of the initial activities of the lesson as a warm-up and leave it at that, or you might delve all the way in and put together a full performance featuring student composition and choreography. Some of these lessons could take place in one class period. Most could be extended to a longer unit, where the strand of the lesson is one part of your class plan.

Thanks

In arriving at this book, I first thank my students, both children and adults, who have inspired me to develop and refine these ideas. I thank my amazing colleagues, Doug Goodkin and Sofia López-Ibor, who have shared the adventure at The San Francisco School and beyond, and who continue to blaze new trails. I thank my own music teachers for inspiring and nurturing my musical creativity, and for equipping me well for the challenges of this path. I thank my parents, Jim and Anne Harding, who supported my love for music from the start and have cheered me on at every twist and turn. I thank my editor, Peter Greenwood, for helping me find the best route to Wobbleton while veering away from vagueness and steering clear of cliché. Finally, I thank my partner, Dan Kluger, who welcomes me home and asks me about my travels.

SPEECH PIECES

Birds of a Feather

Rules

Witches and Watches

Farmer's Almanac

How Many Miles to Babylon?

Planetary Orbits

Friday the 13th

ABOUT SPEECH PIECES

No special equipment required!
In the following activities, the speaking voice and the body are the instruments. Although you might be tempted to skip to the more elaborate instrumental arrangements, I recommend looking into these first examples, for I think they contain the essence of how to work creatively with almost any of the materials in this book. In addition, any of these speech pieces can be extended for work with percussion and melodic instruments.

Rhythmic speech
Language is a wonderful vehicle for rhythm. Words, phrases and sentences in all languages carry natural rhythm, and interesting music can be built from these language materials. Orff and Keetman compiled nursery rhymes, counting rhymes, spells, proverbs, riddles, tongue-twisters, songs and other rich materials in the German language for their original edition of *Music for Children*, and they encouraged each translator to find analogous materials in their own language and culture. I have tried to select (and sometimes create) speech materials that appeal to me both for the musical qualities of the language itself and for the themes and images they evoke.

Natural language accent and meter
In the examples that follow, I have made efforts not to force the words into rhythms, but find the natural rhythms contained in the words. It is important that the musical accent correspond to the emphasized syllables of the words (the acCENT on the right syl-LA-ble?). Nonetheless, it is possible to set any text in a variety of musical meters. For example, most of the settings in duple meter (2/4 and 4/4) could be adapted to compound meter (6/8). Toward the end of this section I give examples of texts that lead to settings in 6/8 (How Many Miles to Bablyon?), polymeter (Planetary Orbits) and additive meters (Friday the 13th).

Rhythmic speech ostinato
An ostinato is a very useful device for creative work with young children in music and movement. These short, repeating musical patterns are quickly mastered by children, and can also be quite easily created by them. Young children who can't yet read can compose their own ostinati rhythms by combining the names of objects. Because ostinati by definition repeat over and over, students can master ostinati quite quickly.

Extending timbre
If a child can speak a rhythmic ostinato accurately to the beat, she can transfer that rhythm to body percussion, un-pitched percussion or to a pitched instrument. Any of these following pieces could be extended from speech into other timbres. The ease of extending rhythmic ideas into the

realm of melody and harmony is one of the most important arguments for the use of the pentatonic scale and drone accompaniments as a musical world for creative work with young children.

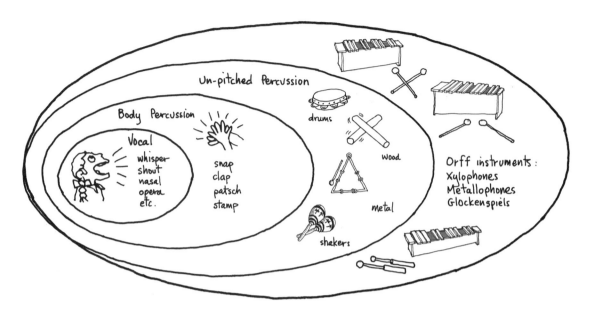

Layered ostinati as composition

Music of a pleasing complexity can be made from layering several ostinati on top of each other.
Some examples of this activity are found in "Rules," and "Birds of a Feather." Creating a group
piece out of ostinati developed by the students is a very satisfying compositional activity. The
teacher's role in this process is to identify the most musically interesting combinations and suggest revisions.

Some rules of thumb for working with student-composed ostinati:

1. **Look for complementary rhythms between ostinati.** Rhythms are *complementary*
   when most beats differ from one another in their rhythmic content and *parallel*
   when most beats are the same in their rhythmic content:

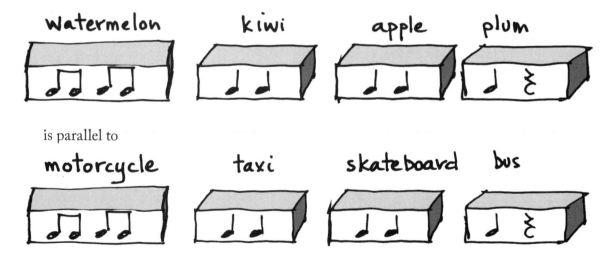

but is complementary to

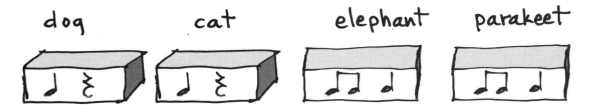

In the case of the first two patterns, I might suggest to the creators of the second pattern to try starting in the middle, resulting in a pattern that is complementary:

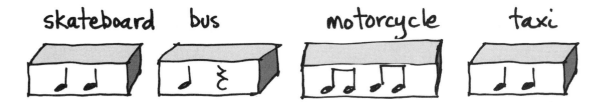

2. **Look for variety and proportion in length.** If all ostinati in a layered texture are the same length (i.e. four beats), the cumulative effect of stacking them will quickly become tiresome to the ear. If, on the other hand, there are some patterns that are twice as long (or half as long), the texture will become more interesting:

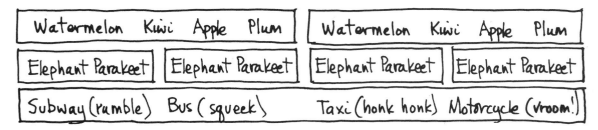

3. **Look out for polymeter.** Often young children will create patterns that vary in meter (i.e. number of beats). For example, to accompany the 4/4 meter rhyme "Birds of a Feather," I invite children to invent an ostinato combining the names of birds. A group comes up with, "Nightingale Hawk Robin."

For experienced students, the overlap of a three-beat and a four-beat pattern can be an exciting challenge (see "Planetary Orbits"), but I find that younger students can hear the other patterns in the texture better if they are in the same meter. So I will often suggest changes that bring the pattern into line with the meter of the poem, for example, repeating the word "Nightingale"

4. **Fight robotic ostinati!** While it is very effective to use language to create rhythmic patterns, there is a danger that these patterns can become unmusical and mechanical, especially when repeated over and over as ostinati. Orff and Keetman encourage the teacher to draw out expressive elements from the words themselves:

> *"See that each word is spoken in such a way that it becomes alive, and concentrate particularly on the sound of each word: "crocus," compared with "fritillary," the sharp sound of "blackthorn" and "buckthorn" in contrast to the legato "winter-heliotrope," the gentle "daffodil" compared with the dark-sounding "rose."**

Drawing attention to other expressive elements of music (timbre, dynamic and pitch) helps create musical interest in ostinati patterns:

Timbre
From the sounds the animals make: hummingbird: hummmmm; crow: CAW!

Pitch
Subway (low); Airplane (high)

---

* Carl Orff and Gunild Keetman, *Orff Schulwerk: Music for Children Volume I* (Margaret Murray Edition) (London: Schott & Co. Ltd, 1957) p.141

Dynamic
Shown in an ostinato with large and small size objects:

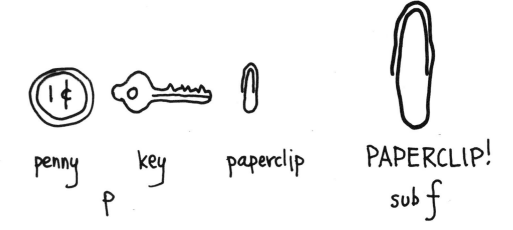

Warning! Beware of ostinitis!

Once you get into the habit of seeing the rhythmic potential of words, watch out! You may find yourself in the supermarket, transfixed by the dairy case "but-ter, half-and-half, one-per-cent, cream!," or honked at by angry cars as you sit in the toll booth, repeating over and over to yourself: "please place your toll in the slot." If this happens to you, you truly have a bad case of ostinitis and should seek immediate medical treatment!

BIRDS OF A FEATHER

An old proverb hatches a speech piece

Birds of a feather
Flock together
Birds of a feather
Flock together
Summertime and wintertime
In every kind of weather
Birds of a feather
Flock together

Play with form of chant
Try out various forms, e.g. AB, BA, ABA, ABB, etc. Introduce form AABA

A

B

Play with the dynamic
Once the students have learned the basic chant in AABA form, introduce the concept of dynamics (loud, soft…) by conducting. Invite students to conduct. Here are some possible signals for forte and piano:

forte
hands wide

piano
hands close

A score with dynamics

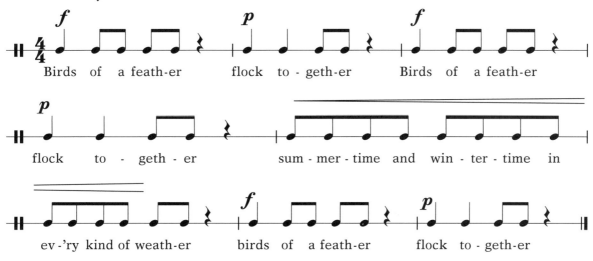

As a canon

I like this chant best as a canon at one measure (second groups starts after two beats). It works nicely with up to four groups.

Sorting birds by rhythm

Have students brainstorm a list of birds, and write them on cards. As a class, sort the birds by rhythm. Try to find at least one example for each of the rhythmic bricks.

Building ostinati

Invite students to work with a partner to create an ostinato using two birds. These can be from the list you have sorted or other birds they know. Each partner chooses one bird, and then together they decide what order to say them in.

I encourage each pair to be able to say their ostinato twice and then clap the rhythm twice. Examples of two-bird ostinati:

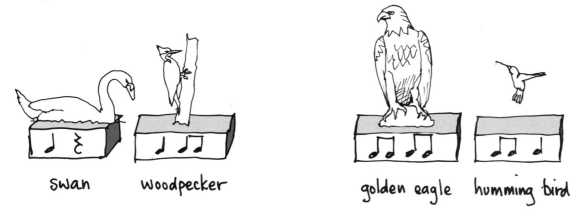

Working with ostinati
- Listen to each ostinato alone. Group repeats each pattern at least twice.
- Listen to two ostinati groups at the same time. Listen for patterns that fit well together.
- Select an ostinato to accompany the "Birds of a Feather" chant. Half the class says the ostinato, other half recites the chant. Switch. Try with two (or more) ostinati simultaneously.
- Have students orchestrate their ostinati using body percussion sounds or un-pitched percussion instruments. Perform chant with body percussion ostinati.
- Challenge students to add dynamic and timbre variations to their patterns. In the examples above, "swan" could become very majestic while "woodpecker" could be staccato, like the sound of a beak pecking. "Golden eagle" might be *forte* to show its size, while hummingbird could be *piano*.

A PERFORMANCE FORM

Introduction
Many birds fly onto the stage, saying their names. They sort into groups by rhythm.

- Unison chant: "Birds of a Feather"
- Chant in canon
- Layering of bird ostinati
- Chant over bird ostinati
- Finale: chant in 4-part canon

Extensions
This piece could engender a larger unit about birds in the classroom. Besides the other bird-themed materials in this book, see the lesson on Saint Saens' "Cuckoo in the Forest" in *Blue is the Sea* by Sofia Lopez-Ibor (Pentatonic Press, 2011).

RULES

A speech piece inspired by a 2nd grade safety unit

"Do unto others as you would have them do unto you"
That is the Golden Rule and at school we have others.

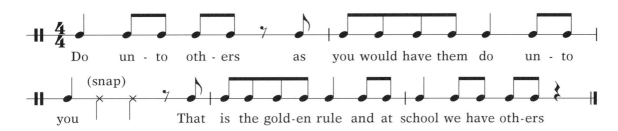

Do un - to oth - ers   as   you would have them do   un - to

you   (snap)   That   is   the gold-en rule and at school we have oth-ers

Play with opposites

The text is in AB form, a perfect system to explore contrast in many elements of music. I set up the exercise by announcing the "Rule of Opposites." I perform the A section, and the students must perform the B section the opposite way.

Pitch—high/low, rising/falling

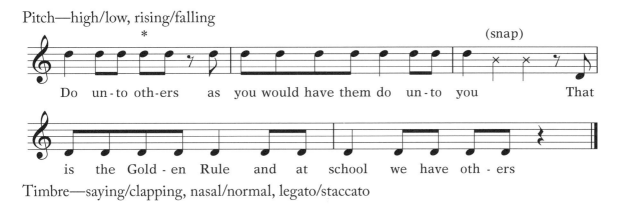

Do un-to oth-ers   as   you would have them do un-to you   That

is   the Gold - en Rule   and   at   school   we   have   oth - ers

Timbre—saying/clapping, nasal/normal, legato/staccato

Dynamic—Forte/piano, crescendo/diminuendo

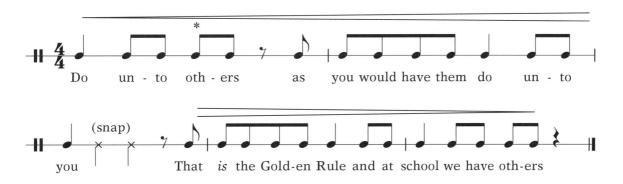

Do   un - to   oth - ers   as   you would have them do   un - to

you   (snap)   That   *is* the Gold-en Rule and at school we have oth-ers

Rhythm- straight/swing

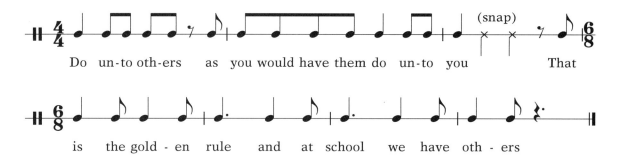

Do un-to oth-ers   as you would have them do un-to you   That

is   the gold - en rule   and   at school   we   have oth - ers

Tempo—Fast/slow, accelerando/ritardando

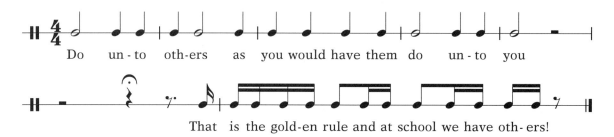

Do   un - to oth-ers   as you would have them do   un - to you

That is the gold-en rule and at school we have oth-ers!

Playing with the form

Invite students to change the form of the text by repeating phrases. The example below repeats "do unto others" and "unto you" three times each:

Do un-to oth-ers,   Do un-to oth-ers,   Do un-to oth-ers,   as

you would have them do   un-to you, un-to you, un-to you   That

is   the Gold - en Rule   and   at school   we   have oth - ers

Try performing as a canon. The word *canon* in music comes from the Latin word meaning "rule;" in other words, a piece of music with special instructions for performance. There are canons by Bach with the rule that one player plays the notes backwards or upside down!* For our purposes, the rules will have to do with how many groups will perform, when they will enter, and how many times they will repeat. The example below shows a canon for two groups at an interval of 4 beats, performed once:

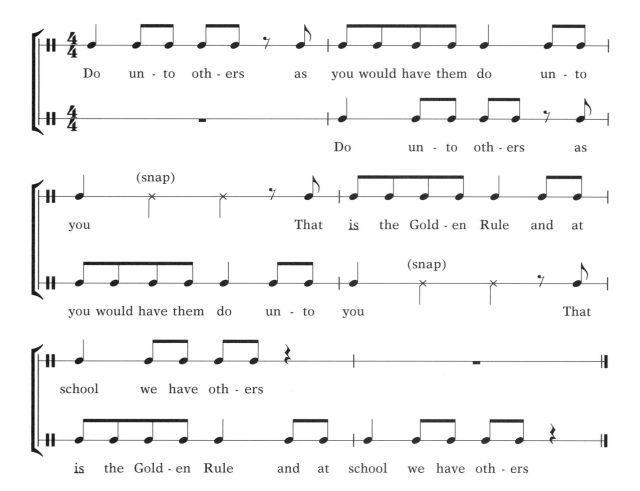

---

* a great visual example of one of Bach's "crab canons" is found in the YouTube film by Jos Leys "Crab Canon by Bach on a Möbius Strip"

Here's an example of a canon at 2 beats, performed by three groups:

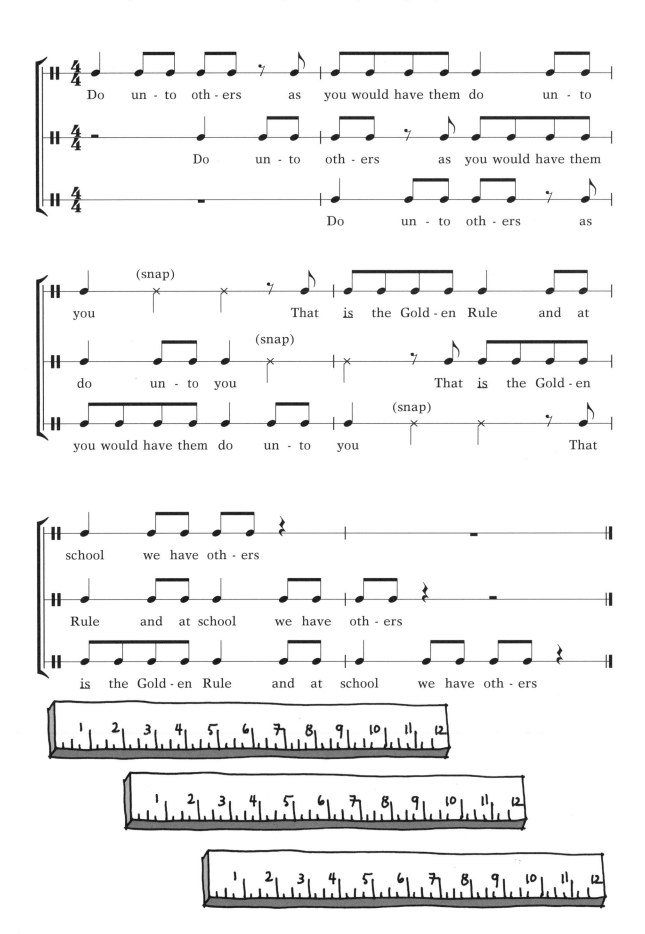

Rule ostinati

Any text can become an ostinato if it is repeated while accompanied by a steady beat. I had the second graders work with partners to think of a rule and learn how to clap its rhythm, trying to keep the same tempo as the chant, "Do Unto Others." Some examples that came from the students:

Composition

Here's an example of the way we put together three of the above ostinati:

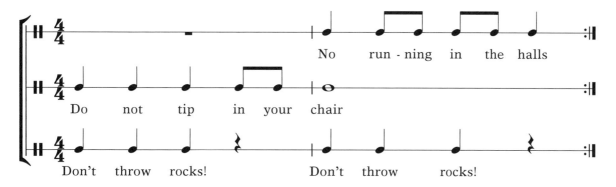

Notice that "Don't thow rocks" repeats every measure, but the other rules repeat every two measures.

To leave more space in the texture, I had "Do not tip in your chair" and "No running in the halls" alternate with the overlap on the word "chair."

Transfer

With the rhythmic ostinato composition in place, we can now play with other timbres. Students can discover ways to play their ostinati using body percussion sounds or on un-pitched percussion instruments. Since this chant is about school rules, you could invite students to explore making rhythms with common objects in the classroom (books, rulers, desks, pencil cases, binders, etc.) Don't forget the rule of treating classroom materials well...

Musical skit

Here's an example of one way to put together a dramatic performance based on school rules:

The First Day of 2nd grade

A new student arrives in the 2nd grade class for her first day. She's excited and nervous, and wants to know what to expect. Her father tells her to remember the Golden Rule: "Do unto others as you would have them do unto you!"

Friendly classmates greet the new student, and all say, in unison:

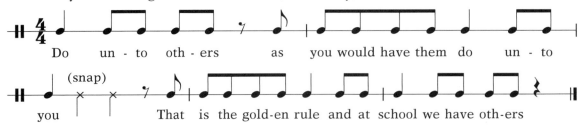

The new student asks, "What are some of the other rules at school?"

Small groups perform their "rule" ostinati, one at a time, explaining each rule and its importance.

New student becomes a conductor, adding ostinati one at a time until all groups are in:

On a signal from the conductor, all groups join together to recite "Do unto others" in unison.

For a grand finale, the entire cast performs the chant in canon, with each "rule" group forming a voice in the canon.

WITCHES AND WATCHES

A tongue-twister speech piece with ostinati

Cartoon caption

Draw a version of the cartoon above, and have students come up with short captions.
Some examples from my third grade students:

> *Witches watching watches*
> *Which watch, witch?*
> *Which watch did the witch watch?*
> *Double double witch witch, Double double watch watch...*
> *Which witch's wrist watch?*
> *Which witch watched which wrist-watch?*

Creating ostinati

Have students make their captions into ostinati, repeating them over a steady beat.

Try out combinations of ostinati.

Try using ostinati to accompany this longer tongue twister[*] (the inspiration for the cartoon):

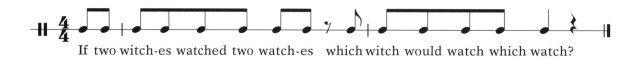

If two witch-es watched two watch-es   which witch would watch which watch?

---

[*]   Joseph Rosenbloom *World's Toughest Tongue Twisters* (New York: Sterling Publishing Co., 1986)

If Two Witches Watched Two Watches

FARMER'S ALMANAC

What's behind a loaf of bread?
Ostinati of folk wisdom accompany a lovely song

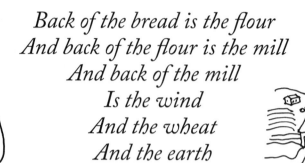

Back of the bread is the flour
And back of the flour is the mill
And back of the mill
Is the wind
And the wheat
And the earth
And the farmer's will

—adaptation of traditional table grace

Lyrics adapted by
James Harding

Traditional English

Back of the bread is the flour   And back of the flour is the mill   And

back of the mill is the wind and the wheat and the earth and the far-mer's will

Teaching the song

The song has a lovely turn of phrase: "Back of the bread is the flour." You can explore this idea literally by creating a set of cards with images or words for bread, flour, mill, wind, wheat, earth, and farmer. As you are introducing the song, flip the front card to the back of the stack to reveal what's behind it...

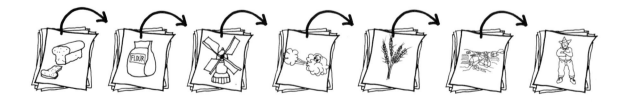

Have kids create gestures for each of the main words. Invite seven students to stand in a line, the first showing "bread" the second showing "flour" and so on.

Variations

Think of another man-made object (or food-stuff) besides bread and make your own sequence. For example, *back of the ice-cream is the milk, and back of the milk is the cow, and back of the cow is the grass, and back of the grass is the earth, and back of the earth is the worm,* etc.

Folk wisdom ostinati

Many languages have phrases that were used by people in the past to remember important things about the seasons, weather, planting, etc. These expressions are rich in history and meaning, and are worth exploring. Many of them also work well as ostinato patterns:

Ring around the moon:
Rain comes soon!

Thirty days hath September, April, June and November.

Clear moon,
Frost soon!

Wind from the east, fish bite the least.
Wind from the west, fish bite the best!

Creating a layered accompaniment

Here's an example of a layering of several folk sayings as an accompaniment for the song.

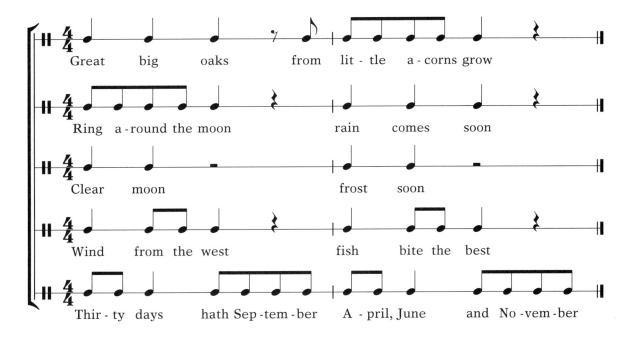

Some ideas for arrangement and further exploration:

Cumulative
Layer in ostinati one at a time. Once all are in, add melody on top. To end, remove ostinati one at a time.

Extensions
I used this arrangement as the introduction to a play of "The Bremen Town Musicians." It established the characters of the farmers whose animals escape and form a band.

Eric Carles' book *Pancake, Pancakes!*[*] explores the ingredients behind making this favorite breakfast treat.

---

[*] Eric Carle. *Pancakes, Pancakes!* (New York: Simon and Schuster, 1992)

HOW MANY MILES TO BABYLON?

This rhyme will get you to 6/8 time (and back again)

How many miles to Babylon?
Three score miles and ten
Can I get there by candle-light?
Yes, and back again!
If your heels be nimble and light
You can get there by candle-light!

What does it mean?

I like the language of this poem, which requires some clarification. A "score" is a measure of twenty, which makes "three score miles and ten" the equivalent of 70 miles. "Can I get there by candle-light?" means "Can I get there before dark?" (the time when candles are lit).

Math game

Students translate number expressions using "score" into modern English numbers. You can make this a rhythmic experience by keeping a beat and chanting the questions and answers. Give a little space for thinking by clapping a rhythmic echo of both question and answer.

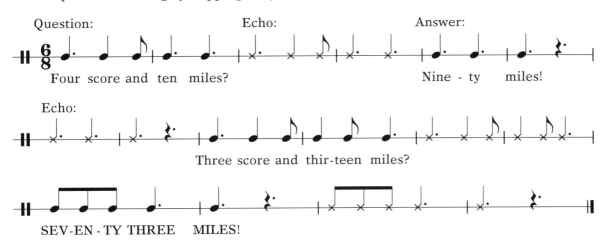

Variations

Have pairs work together on creating a question and answer pattern following the model above. Have each partner choose an un-pitched percussion instrument to perform the echo.

The rhythmic compass

Draw a compass rose wherein each of the four cardinal directions is represented by a different one-measure rhythm in 6/8 time:

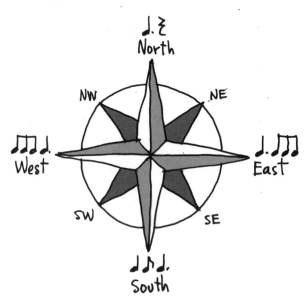

IDEAS FOR WORKING WITH THE RHYTHMIC COMPASS

Cardinal directions

Accompany the rhyme with one cardinal direction ostinato at a time. You could perform these vocally, with body percussion, or with un-pitched percussion. Add lyrics to the rhythms, or use rhythmic syllables:

North   East   Go to the   West is the best!   Way down south

Ordinal directions

For the directions NW, SW, SE, and NE, demonstrate two-measure ostinati:

Combinations

Have small groups create an accompaniment plan for the rhyme. For the first four lines of the poem (the first 8 bars) perform one of the cardinal direction ostinati. For the last two lines (4 bars), switch to an ordinal direction ostinato. Listen to each group's performance and have the other students guess which combination of directions were used.

OTHER IDEAS FOR THE RHYTHMIC COMPASS

Opposite rhythms

Each direction has its opposite on the compass. In this game, the leader plays (and repeats) one of the directional ostinati and the class needs to find and perform the opposite. This game can be played by the teacher with the whole class or by pairs or groups of students. The rhythms could be performed vocally, with body percussion, on un-pitched percussion or on pitched instruments.

Rhythmic navigation

In these activities, the directional ostinati become instructions for movement, either of a person or an object:

Determine which direction is North in the classroom space, and have students react to the rhythms by turning to face the proper direction. Invite student leaders to play the rhythms.

Getting to Babylon

Create a grid either on the board or on the floor and mark the location of "Babylon" and the starting square:

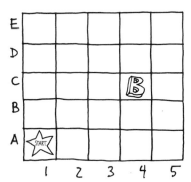

Ask students to come up with a rhythmic combination that will arrive at the Babylon square.

For the puzzle shown, two solutions could be:

East East East North North... BABYLON!

Bab - y - lon!

or North, East, North, East, East... BABYLON!

Bab - y - lon!

Variations

Create a large grid on the floor and use the direction rhythms to move a person through!

Give students their own smaller grids and have them listen to a rhythm and find out where Babylon is.

Example: Starting in square A1, where does the following rhythm put Babylon?

BAB - Y - LON!

Answer: D2

Ideas for performance

Use the rhyme as a rondo theme, with rhythmic episodes featuring the "score" math rhythms and games with the rhythmic compass. The rhyme works well as a two-voice canon at various time intervals, including 2 measures, 1 measure and half measure.

Vehicle variations

Have students choose one "ordinal direction" rhythm from the compass and clap it as an ostinato. The students with the same ostinato form groups. Give each group a card with a form of transportation on it (some ideas below). Groups must use their rhythm from the compass to create a rhythmic scene of their vehicle moving towards Babylon.

For instance, the group's rhythm is: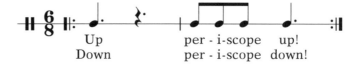

Their transportation is submarine.

They might write lyrics to their rhythm for their submarine travel scene:

They introduce their scene by chanting a variation of the rhyme, subsituting their form of transportation for "candle-light," and creating a rhyming couplet at the end. A possible solution for "submarine":

How many miles to Babylon?
Three score miles and ten.
Can I get there by submarine?
Yes and back again!

If you do not want to be seen
You should go there by submarine.

Can you get there by...motorcar? dragonboat? UFO? bicycle? witch's broom? pogo stick? caravan?

How Many Miles to Babylon?

PLANETARY ORBITS

Polyrhythm and the music of the spheres[*]

earth   venus   mars   jupiter

Earth, Venus and Mars

According to astronomical observation, the relative periods of the orbits of these three planets are:

Earth (1 year)   Venus (.61 years)   Mars (1.88 years)

I expressed the basic proportion of these orbit periods by giving Venus a two-beat phrase; Earth, three-beats; Mars, six:

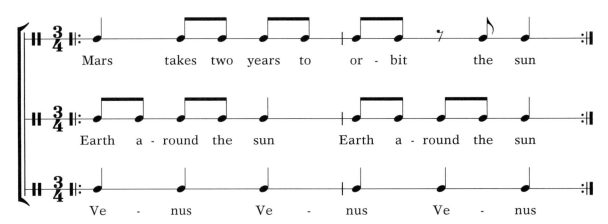

The key to enjoying polyrhythmic textures is to maintain the common beat (quarter notes in this example) in all parts. Playing the beat on a woodblock or drum can help hold the group together.

Extending the ostinati

Create dynamic body percussion patterns for the ostinati.

Play the ostinati on un-pitched percussion instruments with distinct timbres.

Planetary dances

Divide class into three groups, and have each create a circle choreography representing one of the planetary ostinati. These can be very simple (e.g. "Ve-nus" could be moving sideways around

---

[*] Pythagoras, the ancient Greek astronomer and mathematician, used the term "Music of the Spheres" to describe the geometric proportions of distances between the earth and various planets and the sun. The orbital periods of the planets make for a great example of the musical concept of polyrhythm, where patterns of different lengths shift against each other.

the circle with a "side-close" step). For groups with more experience, have the students write down their step patterns using symbols. *

Jupiter

Jupiter's orbital period is about 12 earth years. One musical way to reveal this to the students is for you to improvise 12 measures on hand drum or recorder while they perform their planet ostinati or dances. Ask students to keep track of the number of repetitions they perform before you shout "Jupiter!"

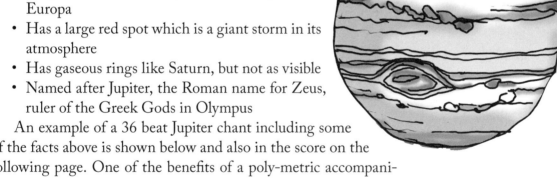

- How many Venus years is Jupiter's orbit? (18)
- How many Mars years? (6)
- How many Earth years? (12)

Once the groups know their correct number, have them perform their dance again while you improvise. Challenge them to join you in shouting "Jupiter!" at the close of the 12-year orbit.

Composing an orbital poem about Jupiter

As a class, compose a rhythmic text about Jupiter that lasts for 12 measures of 3 beats (36 beats). This is a long text, and you'll need lots of facts...

Some facts about Jupiter

- Largest planet in the Solar System
- Fifth planet from the sun
- Jupiter is called a "gas giant" because it is mostly hydrogen and helium
- Surrounded by 63 moons
- Largest moons are Ganymede, Io, Calysto, and Europa
- Has a large red spot which is a giant storm in its atmosphere
- Has gaseous rings like Saturn, but not as visible
- Named after Jupiter, the Roman name for Zeus, ruler of the Greek Gods in Olympus

An example of a 36 beat Jupiter chant including some of the facts above is shown below and also in the score on the following page. One of the benefits of a poly-metric accompaniment is that the text doesn't have to fit one meter.

Accompany Jupiter chant with other planetary ostinati

Challenge the accompanists to listen carefully to the Jupiter chant and end all together saying, "Ju-pi-ter!"

For an introduction, layer the planetary ostinati, starting with Venus, then Earth, then Mars and finally Jupiter. Enjoy the music of the spheres!

---

* For excellent examples of the notation of rhythmic steps, see Gunild Keetman's *Elementaria* (London: Schott, 1974)

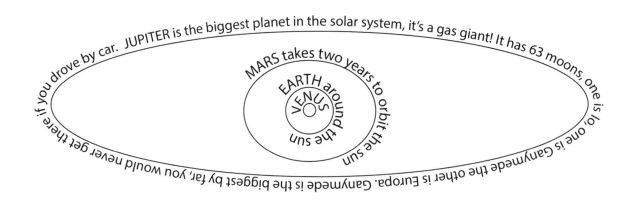

Pentatonic setting on the Orff ensemble

The score below is a transcription of a rhythmic Jupiter text composed by San Francisco School 5th Graders. The melodic ostinati in re-pentatonic mode (see Modes of the Pentatonic Scale) were also composed by the students.

FRIDAY THE 13TH

I wrote this speech piece on Friday the 13th of October, 2006, while teaching at the Orff Institute. If you add up all the numbers of the date (10/13/2006) it comes out to…13!

Breaking a mirror, breaking a mirror,
Very bad luck!
Walk under ladder, walk under ladder,
Very bad luck!
Black cat is crossing, black cat is crossing,
Very bad luck!
Friday the 13th, Friday the 13th,
Very bad luck!

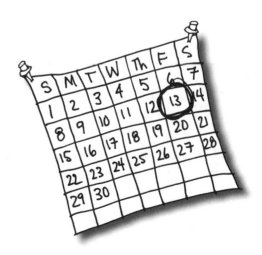

Breaking a mirror...
Walk under ladder...
Black Cat is crossing...
Friday the 13th ...
Very bad, very bad luck!

Friday the 13th

James Harding

Teaching the chant

To introduce the chant, I tell the story of a bad dream I had, showing the class pictures of each bad luck symbol on the way:

> *In my dream, it seemed like a normal day, but as I was brushing my teeth, the bathroom mirror fell…very bad luck! Then I went outside the house and on my way to school I saw a ladder propped up against a house…and I walked under it… very bad luck! Then "Meow!" a cute little black cat ran right in front of me… very bad luck! And then, when I got to school, I looked on the calendar, and it was a Friday, the 13th… very bad luck!*

Practice the four phrases as an echo with the whole group, e.g:

Break-ing a mir-ror, break-ing a mir-ror, ver-y bad luck!

then similarly, "Walk under ladder, walk under ladder, very bad luck!"
"Black cat is crossing, black cat is crossing, very bad luck!" and
"Friday the 13th, Friday the 13th, very bad luck"

Clarifying the meter

Divide into two groups. Group one does "Mirror" and "Black Cat": group two does "Ladder" and "Friday the 13th." Practice the overlapped entrances:

Practice the special ending:

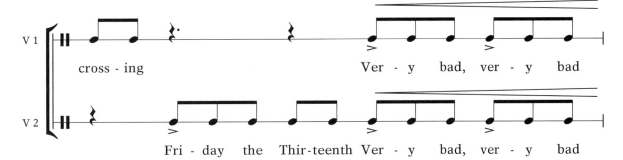

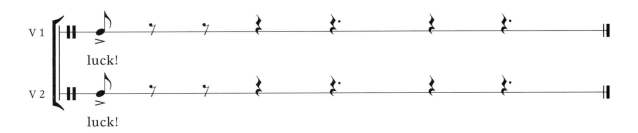

Put the whole chant together, emphasizing the dynamic… starting soft and making a crescendo to a really agitated *fortissimo*!

Extensions for basic chant
Perform on un-pitched percussion instruments. Two-tone instruments like bongos, pairs of congas, agogo bells, timpani and temple blocks work nicely to bring out the groupings of two and three pulses.

Exploring additive meter
The world of meters that combine pulse groupings of 2 and 3 in various ways (additive meter) is an exciting one, and one that is entered quite naturally through speech. The "Friday the Thirteenth" chant could be performed and enjoyed by students without their being aware of the underlying metrical concept. It could also be a jumping off point for a more conscious study of this idea. For this purpose, a system of visual notation combined with speech patterns can be useful. I have used "basketball" to represent the group of three beats and "baseball" to represent the group of two:

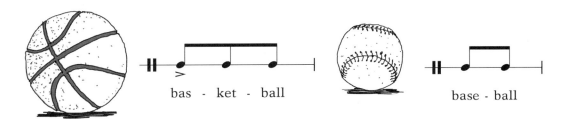

Using these two symbols we can show the basic meter of "Friday the 13th" as:

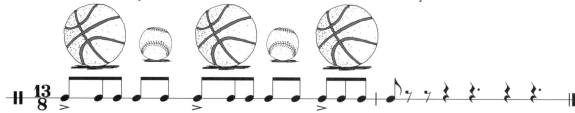

Break-ing a mir-ror, break-ing a mir-ror, ver-y bad luck!

Creating new speech pieces in additive meters

Give students some other good luck/bad luck expressions to create their own speech pieces using additive meter. The topic of luck and superstition is a fascinating one, and there are lots of resources available that describe traditions from all over the world.

Before having students work on their own, it's useful to show them how regular (divisive) meter can be transformed into additive meter. For example, start with this rhyme:

Find a penny pick it up,
All day long you'll have good luck

Start by chanting this in regular meter:

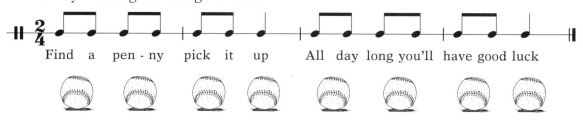

Then show some examples of transformation into an additive meter, such as 7/8:

or 9/8:

Some other luck expressions for creating pieces: *

If you see a spider in the morning, it will bring you good luck.
If you see one at night, bad luck!
—Japan

* an interesting online resource is http://worldsuperstitions.blogspot.com/

If you hear a cat sneeze you will have good luck.
—Italy

Knife falls, gentleman calls;
Fork falls, lady calls;
Spoon falls, baby calls.
(dropping cutlery predicts who will next come to your door)
—England

Never get your hair cut on a Tuesday!
—India

If Candlemas day be fair and clear
There'll be two winters in the year
—Scotland

Opening an umbrella inside is bad luck
—USA

Finding a four-leaf clover is good luck!
—Ireland

If you knock over the salt you will have bad luck
(unless you throw some over your left shoulder)
—various cultures

If you catch a falling leaf in the Autumn
You will have good health in the winter
—England

If you eat warm rice mixed with cold,
the next time you leave the house you will lose your way!
—Thailand

If you see a chimney sweep, grab hold of a button
on your clothes for good luck.
—Poland

Upside-down shoes are signs of bad luck.
—Turkey

Sticking your chopsticks straight up in your bowl of rice is bad luck.
—China

If you hear a cuckoo on the right side of the road, you will have good luck for a year.
-Ireland

Opening and closing scissors without cutting anything is bad luck.
—Egypt

En martes, ni te cases, ni te embarques.
(Don't get married or leave on a trip on Tuesday)
—Spain

SINGING GAMES

WORKING WITH THE VOICE (AND EAR)

The voice as the first musical instrument

The voice is the first musical instrument of most children. So much of the development of the child as a communicator and master of language centers around the use of the voice in relationship with the ear. By a very young age, and without directed instruction, most children have learned to produce and recognize an enormous repertoire of vocal sounds. Working with the voice in music puts this incredible facility to expressive use.

The singing voice

Training young children to perceive pitch patterns and reproduce them accurately with their voices can be effortless or take years, depending on the child. There are many wonderful resources that give ideas on how to develop the singing voice of the child, including much of the Kodaly literature. I have included some important concepts below:

Vocal range

I have tried to pitch all arrangements with children's vocal range in mind (D to shining D!) There are some melodies which go down to middle C or up to high E in the interest of keeping the arrangements compatible with the Orff ensemble. Of course, if the Orff ensemble will not be used, these songs can be taught and performed in any key.

Opportunities to sing alone

The materials that follow provide opportunities for each child to match pitch in the context of a game. It is useful for the child to be able to hear himself without the voices of his classmates, and it is useful for the teacher to hear each child and evaluate how he/she is able to match pitch. Most of the time, I will not choose to correct a child's pitch matching in the context of a game in the interest of keeping it fun and moving along.

Correction

Many adults will tell you a story where they were made to feel bad about their singing voices as a child. The voice is obviously a very personal feature, and many people are quite sensitive to any criticism or correction. It is important to be aware of this when working with children's voices, and to try to be as clear as possible when suggesting changes or corrections that you are not judging or correcting the child herself. The use of puppets and other objects in singing games with young children can help to separate the voice from the child. It may also be better to wait until the end of a class when you can spend some time with the child without her classmates, instead of correcting a child's pitch matching in the midst of a game.

Intervals for ear-training

Two notes that are a major second or more apart tend to be more accurately distinguished by the inexperienced ear, and this is one reason why the early singing games in this book use minor thirds and larger intervals for ear-training purposes. For students having a hard time shifting into their singing voice, an even greater range jump may help them notice and imitate a pitch pattern. In "The Cuckoo and the Eggs," students are challenged to sing the falling minor third in many parts of their vocal range:

Using other children as vocal model

It is often easier for a child to imitate and match another child's singing voice than for her to imitate an adult singing voice. As a male teacher working with young children, I seek out opportunities to have children echo another child's voice in my class. In "Farmer, Farmer," students match pitch with other students with the same grain or seed.

FARMER, FARMER

A singing and listening game

Farm - er, farm - er   Tell me what you're plant - ing

Farm - er, Farm - er,   Tell me what you sow!

Seed sounds

Make four seed-shakers containing different types of seeds or grains. Try to find four grains that produce four distinct timbres when shaken. Transparent containers let the children see the grain within. Make two of each shaker.

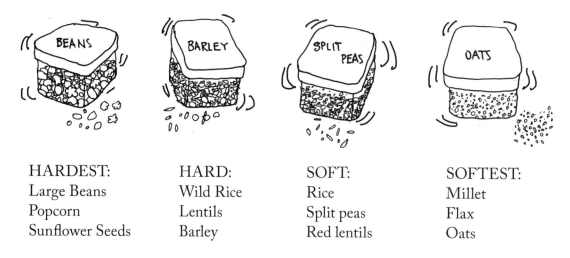

HARDEST:
Large Beans
Popcorn
Sunflower Seeds

HARD:
Wild Rice
Lentils
Barley

SOFT:
Rice
Split peas
Red lentils

SOFTEST:
Millet
Flax
Oats

Demonstrate the four shakers, and tell the students some interesting facts about each grain. Put four of the containers behind your back, and keep the four matching containers in front.

Guessing games

Sing the song and then shake one of the containers behind your back. Have students try to guess which container was shaken by pointing to the matching shaker in front, or naming the grain.

Circle game

Have the children sit in a circle with their hands cupped behind their backs and their eyes closed. While singing the song, distribute the four containers to four children. Children have to figure out which grain/seed they have by shaking it behind their backs. On the next turn, these children stand up and walk around the circle singing the song, passing their containers on to other children in the circle.

Singing game

Add imitative singing to the circle game. You can hold up the matching examples of the shakers as you sing:

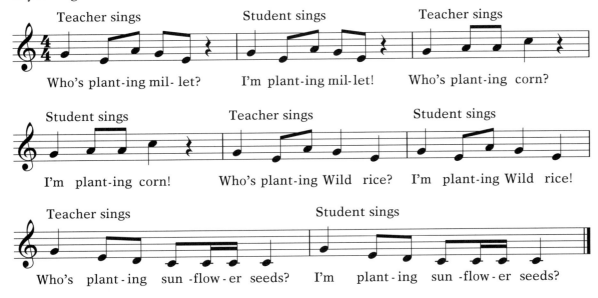

Teacher sings — Who's plant-ing mil-let?
Student sings — I'm plant-ing mil-let!
Teacher sings — Who's plant-ing corn?
Student sings — I'm plant-ing corn!
Teacher sings — Who's plant-ing Wild rice?
Student sings — I'm plant-ing Wild rice!
Teacher sings — Who's plant-ing sun-flow-er seeds?
Student sings — I'm plant-ing sun-flow-er seeds?

Variation:

Pass out all eight of the shakers. Ask one person to sing to find their match, and keep going until all 8 children have sung.

Composing rhythmic patterns

Use the names of the grains to create rhythmic patterns:

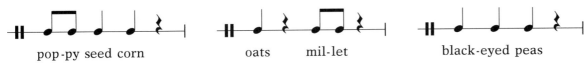

pop-py seed corn   oats   mil-let   black-eyed peas

- Transfer these speech rhythms to body percussion, un-pitched percussion or to the barred instruments.
- Use rhythms to accompany song.
- Create rhythmic scores using real seeds/grains, taped or glued down to a light-colored background:

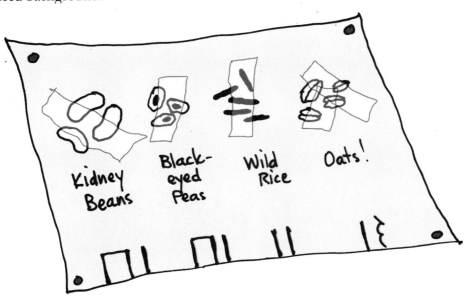

THE CUCKOO AND THE EGGS

Echo, improvisation and a pitch-matching challenge

Cuckoo eggs in other birds' nests

Many European cuckoos are parasitic, laying their eggs in other birds' nests. In this game, one child is the cuckoo and she carries a small basket filled with different-colored eggs (I use sturdy plastic egg-shakers). The other children sit in the circle with their "nests" empty (hands behind their backs, eyes closed). The cuckoo travels around the outside of the circle, putting eggs into other birds' nests, and singing an invented "cuckoo" song, which the other birds echo.

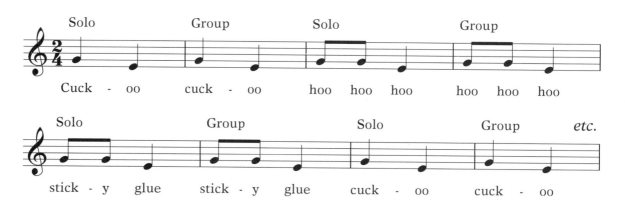

When the cuckoo has given out all the eggs, she puts the empty basket in the center of the circle, singing:

Tossing the eggs back into the nest

All children open their eyes. Those with eggs peek
at the color of their eggs, but keep them hidden. The
teacher (or another student) calls out the colors, and
those with eggs listen for their color and then try to
toss their egg into the central basket. The last egg to
go into the basket (or if none go in, the closest one)
becomes the next cuckoo.

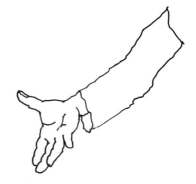

Suggestions for play

This game is an engaging way to work on the skills of accurate pitch matching and to give you
a chance to hear each child improvise vocally within a small range. Some suggestions:

- Teacher models cuckoo. I usually play the role of the cuckoo first, providing examples of staying in the "sol-mi" call and inventing silly words.
- Encourage careful echoing. Draw the children's attention to their amazing ability
  to imitate sounds precisely with their voice—very few animals can do this!
- Reduce the challenge—use a bigger basket, have children sit closer
- Increase the challenge—use a smaller basket, have the children sit farther out in
  the circle, require them to remain seated on their bottoms when they toss.

The cuckoo test: accurate pitch-matching

I like the image of tossing the eggs into the basket as a way of inspiring accurate pitch-matching. After the game is over, I often give the children a "cuckoo test," which means that I hold the basket of eggs high or low and ask them to echo my voice singing "cuckoo" at different pitches. I've found this to be a playful and effective way to assess each child's pitch-matching ability. Often children whose pitch-matching is less developed will echo at a lower tone, so I move down until I match them and then try to move them up.

LOCKS AND KEYS

A singing and movement game inspired by an old joke

I have a gold lock
  I have a gold key
I have a silver lock
  I have a silver key
I have a twisty lock
  I have a twisty key
I have a "mon" lock...

I have a monkey!

Matching

Locks and keys are a great theme to explore in music because they illustrate the concept of precise matching—not every lock fits every key! This can be a compelling image to use when trying to draw your students' attention to precise matching of pitch or physical shape.

Lock and key cards

Create a set of matching lock and key cards. For young children beginning to read, it's helpful to put the full text on the card along with the image, such as:

Some possible locks and keys:
Colors: red, blue, green, yellow, purple, etc.
Patterns: striped, spotted, solid, etc.
Jokes: mon-key, don-key, tur-key

Pitch matching game

Shuffle the lock and key cards, and pass them out in the circle. One person sings the lock card, and the person with the corresponding key card has to match the melody. Melodies can be simple "sol-mi" chants (as in the example below) or be improvisations in the full pentatonic scale. Teacher modelling can establish the basic vocabulary, and then "lock" singers should be encouraged to improvise their own melodies. "Key" singers should be encouraged to match as precisely as possible, paying attention not only to pitch but to dynamic, tempo, articulation, and timbre as well:

Variations of pitch matching game

Variation	Useful for...
Teacher sings locks, whole class sings keys	Modelling ideas, warm-up.
Pass out the key cards only. Teacher sings locks and individual students sing keys.	Assessing individual students' ability to match pitch.
Pass out the key cards only. Select one student to sing the lock cards.	Using a strong student singer as a model.
Pass out the lock cards. Individual students sing locks and teacher sings keys.	Teacher modelling precise matching.
Pass out lock cards. Individual students sing locks and one student sings keys.	Challenge for a strong singer. Encourages variety for "lock" singers.
Pass out both lock and key cards. Individual students sing locks and partners answer.	Fun way to pair up students for partner work.

Complementary shapes

Keys have to fit locks exactly, with the "teeth" of the key fitting into precise spaces within the lock. Have students work with the idea of positive and negative space in reacting to their partner's shape.

In partners, with one student being the "lock" and the other being the "key."

Accompanied by the chant below, "locks" move out into the space and freeze on the word "LOCK!" trying to create an interesting shape with defined spaces.

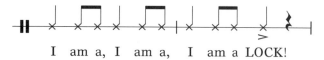

"Keys" then follow their partners out into the space, creating a shape that fills in the spaces of the lock (without touching):

I am a, I am a, I am a KEY!

FEATURING PROPS

From Wibbleton to Wobbleton

Boxes

Diddle Diddle Dumpling

Betty Botter

Fortune Teller/ Roses are Red

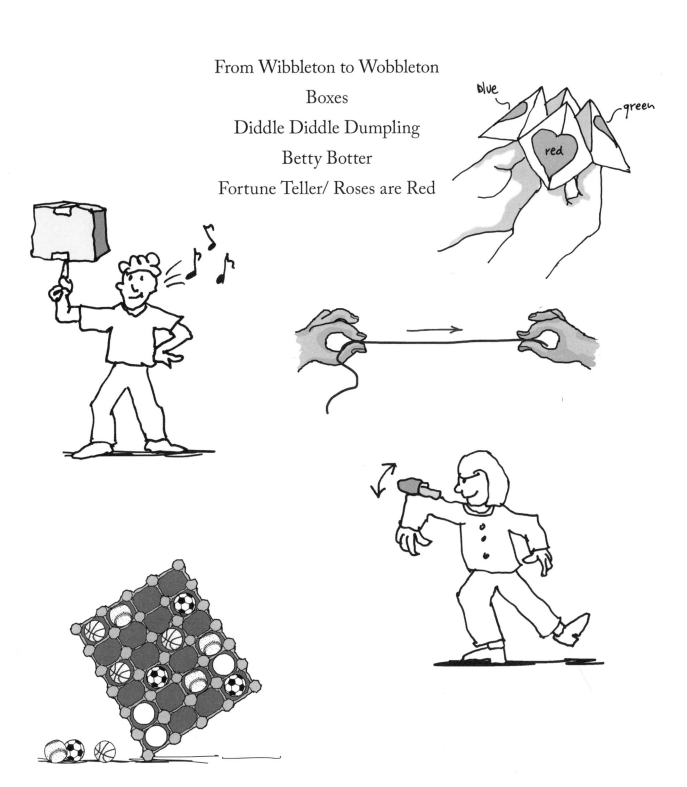

WORKING WITH PROPS

These next five lessons are built around exploring music using specific materials: yarn, cardboard boxes, egg cartons and ping-pong balls, house slippers, and paper fortune-tellers. In this area, I have been hugely inspired by my colleague Sofía López-Ibor, who introduced me to the habit of thinking expansively about common objects for the purposes of teaching music. When she herself was a student at the Orff-Institute in Salzburg looking for a topic for her thesis, Dr. Hermann Regner advised her to study the contents of her trash can for a week, and select one object to explore as a tool for teaching music. She chose a cardboard tube and wrote over 500 pages! While these lessons are smaller in scope, I hope that they will inspire you to think of your own uses of these materials and others. Here are some suggestions of ways of thinking about props and their uses in the music classroom.

How can I use this prop to explore the elements of music?

It can be helpful to make a chart as a way of brainstorming...

Prop	Pitch	Rhythm	Form	Dynamic	Timbre	Tempo
paper plate	giant note heads!	each plate is a beat! ①⊓③ draw	draw A, B, C etc. ⒶⒷⒶ	little + big plates ○ ◯	play them scrape strike + shake	FAST SLOW

Special benefit: seamless transitions! Organizing a lesson around a prop is a way to keep continuity and flow while moving between a variety of activities...

How can I use this prop to connect the students with each other?

Can the students share one prop? Can it be passed back and forth or around in the circle?

How can I use this prop to encourage creative work?

Can the prop become a building block that students can construct with or rearrange? Can it become a prop in a dramatic scene?

How can the prop inspire movement exploration?

Can students move with it? Can they balance it on different body parts? Can they use it as an object to move around? Can it be used to give movement ideas (images or words drawn on it, for example)?

Do I have room to store this prop?

If you're like me, I never ask myself this question until it's too late...

FROM WIBBLETON TO WOBBLETON

Welcome to the title lesson, where string is the thing. Here, yarn is used to explore melodic and harmonic ideas, along with geometry and map-making.

From Wibbleton to Wobbleton is fifteen miles
From Wobbleton to Wibbleton is fifteen miles
From Wibbleton to Wobbleton,
From Wobbleton to Wibbleton,
From Wibbleton to Wobbleton is fifteen miles

Introduce the text

> *"Once there were two towns. One was called Wibbleton and the other was called Wobbleton. There was a road between the towns that was 15 miles long. So...from Wibbleton to Wobbleton is...? From Wobbleton to Wibbleton is...? What about from Wibbleton to Wobbleton and back to Wibbleton? What about from Wobbleton to Wibbleton to Wobbleton to Wibbleton?"*

Clarify form with body percussion

Have class learn this body-percussion pattern in partners, where "Wibbleton" is always accompanied by touching palms with partner and then clapping your own hands, "Wobbleton" is always accompanied by a patsch and a clap, and "fifteen miles" is always accompanied by three stamps, as shown in the score below:

Travelling rhyme

Fly to another partner when you hear this travelling rhyme. Make the sounds of the crows (Caw! Caw!) in the rests (* *). When the travelling rhyme is done, practice "From Wibbleton to Wobbleton" with your new partner.

It's only ten miles as the crow flies **
It's only ten miles as the crow flies **
    In blue skies **
    With yellow eyes**
    It's only ten miles!

Making variations

Have the students create a variation of the clapping play, either with a partner or in a group of four. Have them substitute their own ideas for motions for "Wibbleton," "Wobbleton" and "Fifteen Miles." (see "Which Came First?" for a similar activity substituting gestures for repeating words).

Rondo form performance

Chant the travelling rhyme as a rondo theme in between the "Wibbleton to Wobbleton" variations performed by the student groups.

Putting the rhymes together

Have half the class chant "Wibbleton to Wobbleton" and the other half chant the "Travelling Rhyme," as indicated in the score below:

Preparing the material

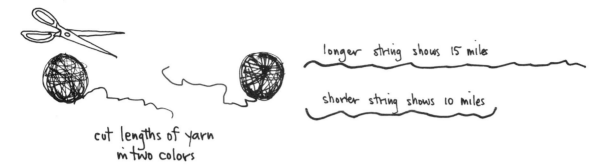

cut lengths of yarn
in two colors

longer string shows 15 miles

shorter string shows 10 miles

Phrasing and breathing

Give a length of yarn to each student. This could be as a reward for their fantastic performance of "Wibbleton to Wobbleton" and the "Travelling Rhyme!"

Have students practice the technique of pulling the yarn through the thumb and forefinger of one hand until the end pops through.

- Now try to make the yarn last for as long as the first phrase of the poem ("From Wibbleton to Wobbleton is fifteen miles")
- Try the second phrase
- Try the third phrase—"From Wibbleton to Wobbleton, From Wobbleton to Wibbleton, From Wibbleton to Wobbleton is Fifteen Miles." Notice the longer phrase and how the yarn needs to be played out more slowly.
- Can you recite the whole poem on one "string" (one breath)?
- Can you sing/chant the poem on a single, steady tone on one breath?
- Do you run out of breath sooner when you sing or when you chant?
- What can you do to make your breath last longer when you sing?

Pulling yarn through pinched fingers is a very pleasant sensation, and a great tactile metaphor for the kind of muscular control needed to regulate steady breathing in singing and wind instrument technique. For string teachers, it can also relate to bowing.

This is a great opportunity to review some elements of vocal technique, such as good posture, deep and silent preparatory breath, use of the diaphragm, dynamic control, etc.

Movement exploration

"As the crow flies" means a straight line from point to point. Have students explore moving through space while keeping their lines straight (yarn taut). You can accompany their movement with your own improvised music, with silence, or with recorded music. Encourage students not to talk, but to enjoy the movement without words...

Horizontal lines

Explore high and low levels

Vertical lines

Can your line be an axis that you spin around?

Can you be the axis that your line spins around?

Diagonal lines

Explore upward and downward motion.
Paddling a canoe...

Parallel lines

Parallel lines never touch!
Try being parallel with someone without their knowing.
Parallel movement far away and close together.
One line is high and the other is low.

Perpendicular lines

An interesting challenge!

Maps for singing and listening and composing

Find a partner with a different length string from you (other color). Create a map on the floor of the Wibbleton to Wobbleton situation. The shorter string is straight "as the crow flies"—between the two towns. The longer string is the real road, which has curves and turns and twists and may cross over the straight line:

These maps may become musical scores. Some ideas:

- Sing the map with your partner, where the straight line is the drone pitch and curving line is the melody. A possible interpretation of the map on the previous page is shown below:

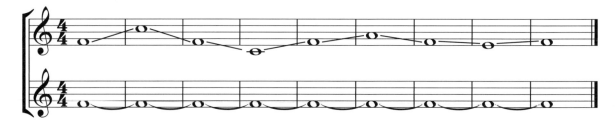

- Notice when the lines cross and listen for your voices coming together into unison.
- The curved line can be sung like a siren (sliding up and down pitch).
- The curved line can be sung in a musical scale.
- The straight line could be sung as a single, sustained note.
- The straight line could be sung on one note but with rhythm.

Listening

With your partner, form a map to represent the music you hear. What map would you make if you heard this example, for instance?

Making more permanent maps

After the above explorations, you may want to have your students glue their yarn down to paper to form a permanent map, which they can decorate with more details, add a scale, a compass rose, etc.

Other map extensions

For math challenges, add (or have class add) other towns, roads and distances to the map:
From Warbleton to Waggleton is…?
From Warbleton to Wobbleton is…?

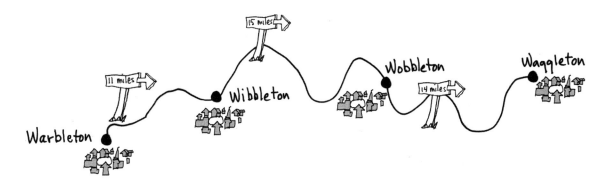

Three-part arrangement

The map below can help in teaching my three-part choral arrangement of "From Wibbleton to Wobbleton." The first sopranos take the high road back and forth. The second sopranos stick to the drone note. The altos take the low road on the "Travelling Rhyme."

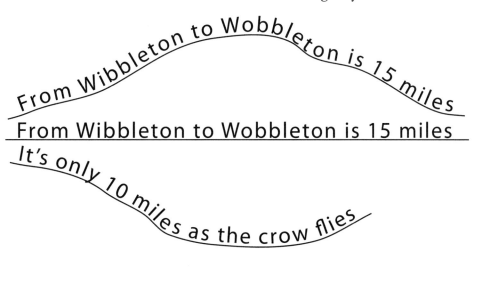

From Wibbleton to Wobbleton

Mother Goose Rhyme
Setting and Lyrics by
James Harding

BOXES

A great object to play with in the music classroom!

Preparing the material

For these activities, I use one-foot cubic cardboard boxes (12"x12"x12"). These are available in the U.S. from office supply stores, and, less expensively, from direct-shipping supply companies online. I usually make a set of 20–25 boxes. I look for cardboard-colored, matt tape to seal them. I tape the flaps closed to form cubes. This is best done with two people: one to hold the flaps closed and the other to apply the tape. Ask for help!

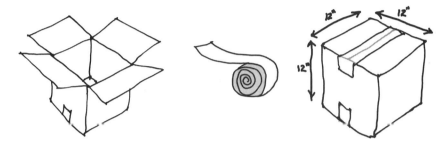

I then decorate them, sometimes quickly with marker, sometimes more carefully with stencils.

Decoration for the activities on the following pages

16 boxes decorated with instrument images on two opposite sides and quarter notes and eighth-note couplets on two other opposite sides (see following pages for images). One box will have a quarter rest on both sides. You will have room on the top and bottom sides to draw any other useful patterns, or leave them blank.

1 box with the six elements of music:

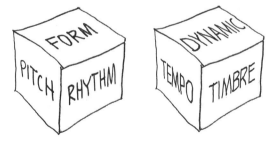

2 boxes with the Laban effort shapes (see following pages):

BUILDING

Susie is a carpenter, a carpenter, a carpenter
Susie is a carpenter, all day long
She works in the morning
She breaks at noon
She works in the evening, all day long! *

Pile a bunch of boxes (I use 16 for the following activities) in front of the class. Challenge individual students to build structures in the time it takes to sing the song. After the song is done, ask them to describe what they've built to the class... "It's a castle!" "It's two skyscrapers" "It's an arm-chair." Invite another student to add to the structure or dismantle it and build something else. The song says "She breaks at noon" (with a fermata on noon!): have builders stop their work at that moment in the song.

Building variations
- Single builders: one student builds something and then describes it to the class.
- Teams: two builders work at the same time without talking.
- Wall/tower of specific dimensions: ask students to build a wall 2 boxes high along it's length.
- A pyramid: what is the largest pyramid you can build with 16 boxes?
- A cube: what's the largest cube you can build?
- Parallel building from two piles: divide the boxes into two equal piles and invite two builders to work at the same time. One is the "master carpenter" and the other is an "apprentice." The apprentice must copy what the master builds.

Susie is a Carpenter

James Harding
(based on Ella Jenkins
"Hammer Hammer Hammer")

Su - sie is a car - pen - ter, a car - pen - ter, a car - pen - ter
Su - sie is a car - pen - ter All day long She works in the morn - ing She
breaks at noon She works in the eve - ning All day long!

* Song adapted from Ella Jenkens "Hammer, Hammer, Hammer" found on *Little Johnny Brown* Smithsonian Folkways, 1991)

Wall of timbres

Build a wall of boxes and hide percussion instruments behind it. Decorate the boxes with the pictures and names of the instruments: this helps students to see the possibilities of what they are hearing in the game.

Who's That

Appalachian, traditional

Who's that tap-ping at my win-dow Who's that knock-ing at my door?

Listening and echoing game variations

- One student goes behind wall and claps a rhythm—group echoes back.
- A student goes behind the wall and plays a rhythm on one of the sixteen instruments—class echoes.
- Two students go behind wall. Class keeps steady beat while the two instruments jam together. Can you tell which two instruments are playing?
- Three or more students go behind wall…
- Timbre families: players leave out one timbre family (wood, metal, skin or shakers) Can you guess which family is missing?
- Mystery instrument: there is no picture of this one… can you guess what it is?

Reading rhythms

Create a wall of boxes showing the rhythmic elements of quarter note, eighth-note couplet, and quarter-note rest. You can transition easily from the last activity by just swivelling the columns one quarter turn (see "Preparing the Material" at the beginning of this lesson).

Reading pathways

Young children learning to read and write words and letters usually find rhythmic notation quite easy in comparison. In these examples, only three symbols need to be mastered and named. For this reason, it's quite possible to play with reading rhythms in many different pathways, not just conventional left to right.

Start with conventional, Western left-to-right reading.

   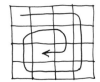

- In the Middle East, written language is often read left to right.
- In many Asian languages, written language starts at the top right and is read in columns.
- What about reading on other planets? Challenge your students to find other pathways where each box gets read only once.
- Many paths at once: have everyone choose their own path and perform it at the same time at the same tempo. Can you get a clean ending?
- Rests out loud: perform your pathway again, this time making a vocal sound instead of the rest. Try performing your pattern in silence except for the rest, which is still a vocal sound. Have the whole class perform their patterns this way at the same time, enjoying hearing the rests popping up all around.

Other musical elements with pathways

In addition to reading rhythm, encourage students to imagine other musical parameters that could be suggested by their pathways:

Dynamic

Higher level boxes could be louder, lower level softer.
Accents could happen at the start of each line, or at the corners of the path.

Pitch

Higher boxes could be higher pitch, lower boxes lower pitch.

Timbre

Each level could have its own body percussion timbre, e.g. stamp, pat, clap, snap.

Guessing game

Have one student perform her pathway and have the class try to guess what it is. The added musical elements will help give clues.

Other structures for the rhythmic boxes

When I gave third grade students some time to create other structures for reading rhythms from the boxes, they came up with some fun ones:

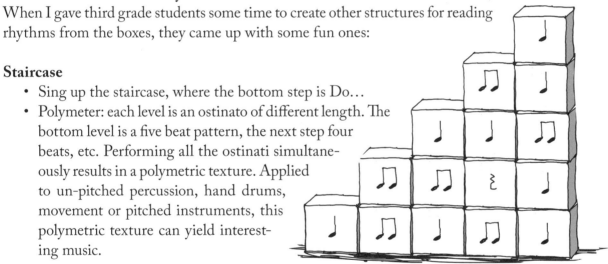

Staircase

- Sing up the staircase, where the bottom step is Do…
- Polymeter: each level is an ostinato of different length. The bottom level is a five beat pattern, the next step four beats, etc. Performing all the ostinati simultaneously results in a polymetric texture. Applied to un-pitched percussion, hand drums, movement or pitched instruments, this polymetric texture can yield interesting music.

Pathway

- Placing the boxes into a pathway on the floor creates a linear rhythm which can be performed by straddling the path and reading as you pass over each box.
- Try forward and backward.
- Try performing the rhythm in a canon… follow the leader!

WHAT'S INSIDE?

Work song steady beat

- Unload the boxes from the stack with a hearty sea chanty or other work song.
- Have students keep the beat on the side of the box with both hands by tossing lightly and catching.
- Encourage students to pass boxes safely by making eye contact with someone before they pass to them.
- Once all the boxes are in students' hands, try slowing down and speeding up the tempo.

Movement and drama game: What's in the box?
In this game, the teacher says what's in the box and the students have to show the contents with dramatic movement. Use an audible instrument to signal a freeze.

Move as if your box was filled with:

Feathers!

Lead bricks!

Helium!

Something sticky

Something rotten!

Super magnet!

Fragile!

Superballs!

Surprise gift

Live animal!

What else?

The musical marketplace

Have students imagine something in their box that they can sell in the market. Ask them to invent a market call to catch the ear…

How can you make your call stand out?

While you walk in the market place, see if you can find out about 3 other things for sale while making your own call.

Singing improvisation game

Teacher sings question to one of the sellers in the market, and the seller tries to sing back an answer, improvising with the same set of pitches:

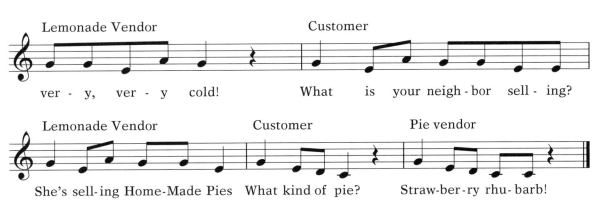

Market call compositions

Have the market vendors form a big circle, facing the center.

Choose three to six market calls near one another and listen to them all call at once for a few seconds.

Ask the other students to notice which calls they could hear clearly? This is a good time to re-mind students of the elements of music (you could decorate a box with all six)—Dynamic ("It was the loudest!") Pitch ("I could hear them singing their call in a high voice.") Timbre ("They whistled at the end.") Rhythm ("They kept the beat on their box.") Form ("They changed their call when they repeated it.") Tempo ("They accelerated!").

After you have heard all the small groups, have each group keep working together to create a composition where all of their calls can be heard clearly.

Here's an example, where the students are layering their market calls as ostinati:

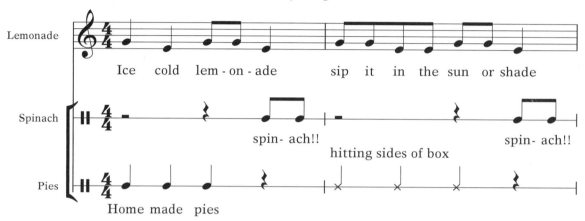

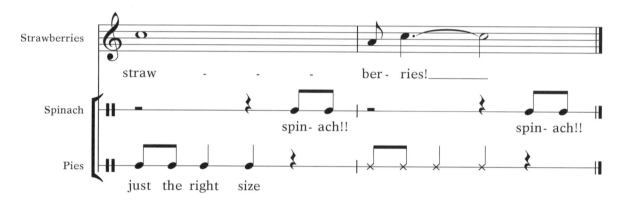

Another example, where the students have added an introduction and then say all their products in sequence:

Have groups perform their compositions, and have listeners appreciate what they heard, using musical vocabulary.

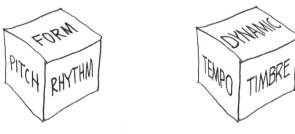

There are several famous examples of musical compositions featuring market calls. The introduction of "Who Will Buy?" from "Oliver!" is a favorite. The round "Chairs to Mend" is another. The last movement of Haydn's Symphony 104 is based on a market call.

Movement composition

Decorate two boxes with the Laban Effort Shapes, dividing them into light and strong categories. Have students work on a movement composition featuring one gesture from each box. Students roll the boxes like dice to receive their two movement ingredients at random.

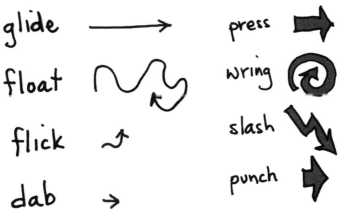

Remind students of some options

- Movements could happen sequentially or simultaneously
- Movements could be repeated or happen just once
- Movements could be expressed by the whole body or by any parts of the body

Remind the students to emphasize contrast

Can you make the light movements truly light? Can you make the strong movements strong?

Further extensions:

Sound accompaniment

You could have the group add vocal sounds to accompany their movements.
You could have another group accompany with vocal sounds or with instrumental sounds (unpitched or pitched).

Variations
Divide the gestures differently, according to duration or pathway:

A boxy diagram of the Laban effort shapes *

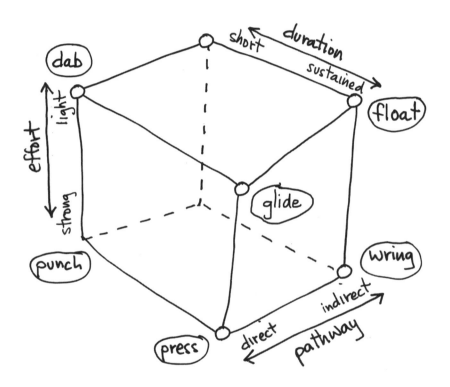

Working with this vocabulary will enable you to increase the expressive range of your students' movement ideas.

These descriptive terms are from the work of Rudolf von Laban and are described in greater detail in his book, *The Mastery of Movement*, MacDonald and Evans, ISBN 0 7121 1287 1

---

* This diagram was inspired by a similar illustration by Luciana Soares Santos in *Criandança* by Daraina Pregnolatto (Brasilia: LGE Editoria, 2004) p. 61

DIDDLE DIDDLE DUMPLING

Don't wait for the other shoe to drop... use it to teach music and movement!

Diddle Diddle Dumpling, my son John
Went to bed with his trousers on
One shoe off, one shoe on
Diddle Diddle Dumpling, my son John

Passing shoes

Each child in the circle holds one shoe: someone else in the circle has its pair. Pass the shoes to the person to your right on the accented beats in the rhyme:

Did-dle, did-dle dump-ling my son John   Went to bed with his trous-ers on

One shoe off,   one shoe on   Did-dle, did-dle dump-ling my son John

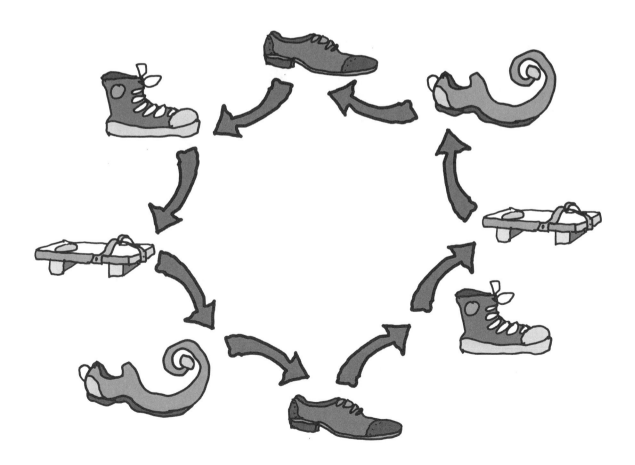

Shoe matching

At the end of the chant, everyone holds onto the shoe they received on the last beat. Teacher holds up shoe and sings, "Who has my shoe?" Student with matching shoe sings back "I have your shoe," trying to match the melody of the teacher.

Variations

Teacher sings "Who has my shoe?" In this role, teacher can model a variety of simple melodies to copy:

Student sings "Who has my shoe?" Choose a strong singer to improvise the melodies for others to copy.

Pass leadership. The person who answers "I have your shoe" is the next one to sing "Who has my shoe?"

Slippers

Inexpensive house-slippers can be ideal for some extensions of this game. Sometimes you can find matching colors and patterns, or you can create your own matching pairs by drawing symbols on the toes:

Rhythm reading

Slip a card with a four beat rhythm pattern into each slipper and pass slippers to the poem. When passing stops, have each student take out the rhythm and place it on the slipper like a music stand for reading practice:

Variations on rhythmic reading

- Each student reads his or her pattern out loud, one at a time around the circle.
- Students read their patterns all at the same time, repeating four times.
- All students with green slippers read their patterns, all students with orange slippers, etc.
- Students with matching slippers combine their patterns into an 8 beat rhythm.
- Use rhythms to accompany the chant "Diddle Diddle Dumpling."
- Apply rhythms to body percussion, un-pitched percussion or as borduns on the barred instruments.

Movement ideas with slippers

During these exercises, teacher could accompany by playing the rhythm of the rhyme on a percussion instrument, experimenting with tempo, accent, dynamic and timbre changes to create signals for stopping, starting, direction and level change, etc.[*]

Body part isolations

Put slipper on one foot. Explore moving the slipper in space, keeping your balance on the other foot; put slipper on the other foot. Put the slipper on one hand: put slipper on the other hand.

Balance

Balance the slipper as you move without holding onto it. On the palm of your hand. On the back of your hand. Your elbow. Your knee. Your back. The top of your head.

Pathway

Put the slipper on the floor, and use it as a space marker.

    Walk around your slipper; change directions on a musical signal.

    Jump over your slipper—forward, backward, sideways.

    Make a figure eight around your own and someone else's slipper.

    Make a pathway in the room that links all the same colored slippers.

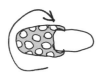   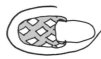 

With partner

Move with the slippers held between your bodies—don't let the slippers fall! Between you and your partner's: hand, elbow, hip, back, forehead, ear, shoulder, bottom, belly, feet!

---

[*] For many ideas about movement exploration and reaction training, see Gunild Keetman *Elementaria* (London: Schott, 1974)

Make a balanced shape with your partner where the slipper foot is not touching the ground!

Drama

Pretend the slipper is not a slipper but something else (a kitten, a catcher's mitt, a stylish hat, a phone, a plate of fancy food, etc.) and show what it is with your movement. Have the class watch and guess.

A Stitch in Time

James Harding

Traditional
("Down the Ohio")

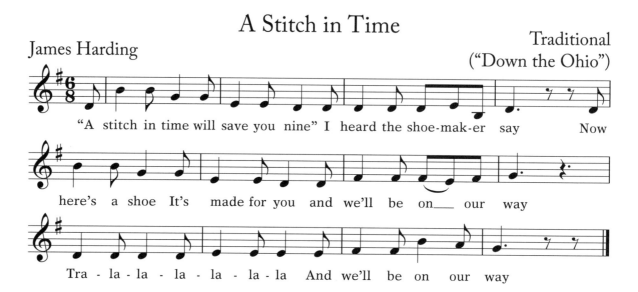

"A stitch in time will save you nine" I heard the shoe-mak-er say   Now

here's a shoe It's made for you and we'll be on___ our way

Tra - la - la - la - la - la-la And we'll be on our way

Shoemaker dance game

I adapted this from a traditional social dance game that I learned from Sanna Longden.* The tune is from an old American playparty "Down the Ohio."

- Students form a longways set (two lines facing one another with a "street" in-between).
- At the head of the set, three chairs.
- One dancer is the shoemaker, holding a shoe or slipper and sitting in the center chair.
- The first two dancers from the other team sit on either side of the shoemaker; these are the customers.
- On "Now here's a shoe, it's made for you" the shoemaker hands the shoe to one customer (figure 1).
- On "...and we'll be on our way" the shoemaker joins hands with the other customer, and on the "tra-la-la" the shoemaker and the customer sashay down the street, going to the end of their team's line (figure 2).

customer   shoemaker   customer

---

* Sanna Longden is based in Chicago and teaches folk dance to people of all ages. The "Paddle Dance" (French Canadian) is found in her collection *More Favorite Folk Dances* (Folkstyle Productions)

- Meanwhile, the customer with the shoe becomes the new shoemaker, and two new customers from the other team sit at his/her side (figure 3).

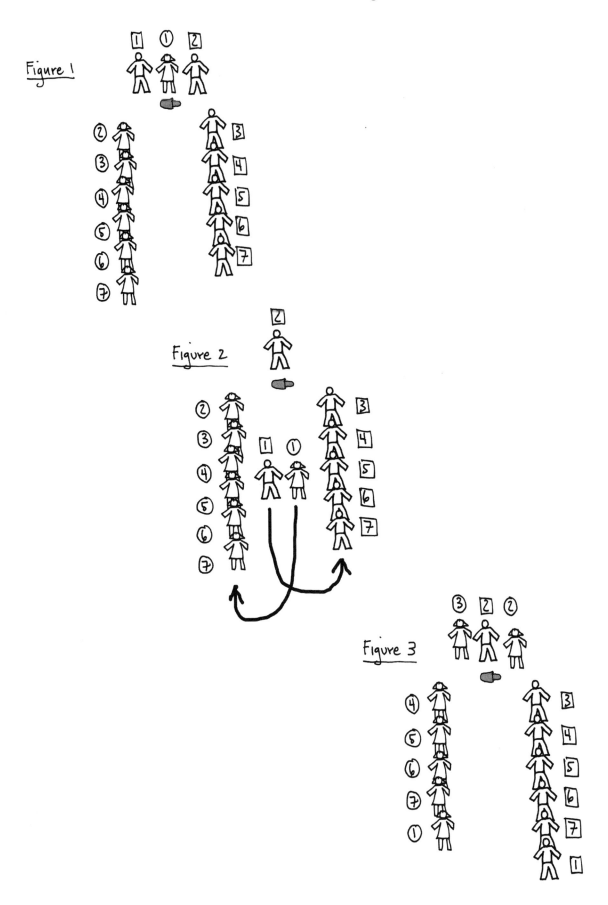

BETTY BOTTER

Better batter thanks to Oriol Ferré's egg carton ideas[*]

butter

Betty Botter bought some butter
"But," she said,"this butter's bitter!
If I put it in my batter
It will make my batter bitter;
But a bit of better butter,
That would make my batter better"

bitter

batter

So she bought a bit of butter
Better than her bitter butter
And she put it in her batter
And her batter was not bitter
So 'twas better Betty Botter
Bought a bit of better butter!

better

Ping pong ball timbres

As a prelude to this lesson, introduce ping pong balls as representations of different timbres. I have found ping pong balls decorated as various sports balls (basketballs, soccer balls, baseballs) and in various colors. You can also decorate plain ping-pong balls yourself. For this lesson we need four distinct timbres.

 Clap Stamp "Whooo"  ?

Clap when I catch the basketball

Toss the ball up and catch it again. Class has to clap whenever you catch it. Try longer and shorter throws to keep everyone alert.

Stamp when I catch the soccer ball

Same game but with stamping.

Two timbres at once

Ideas: alternate hands, sustain one timbre while you throw the other, switch

[*] Oriol Ferré teaches in Barcelona, Spain, and is a trombonist, juggler and magician, as well as the director of a music school. Look out for future publications of his pedagogical ideas. I thank him for his permission to develop and present these ideas with egg cartons and ping pong balls.

Vocal timbre

Follow arc of the baseball as it goes up and back down on a vocal sound like "wooooo."

Make up a fourth timbre

Ask students to come up with a fourth timbre for the last ball.
Review all four timbres (juggling skills will come in handy!)

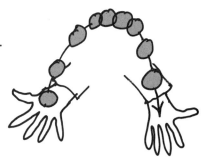

Egg cartons-preparing the material

For the activities that follow, you will need seven egg trays. Egg trays are the restaurant size egg cartons for 30 eggs, and you can find them easily at any local breakfast place. Cut one of the trays down to 24 chambers (6X4) for the first part of the lesson below.

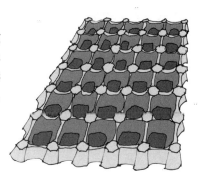

Four beat ostinato

Use just the top four chambers of the egg carton. Place one ball in the first chamber and conduct a four beat ostinato by pointing to each chamber. The empty chambers are rests.

Have a student add another timbre into one of the empty chambers and have the class perform the resulting ostinato. Add a third and fourth timbre.

Practice performing these four beat ostinati as an accompaniment to the rhyme Betty Botter.

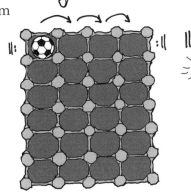

Random accents

Using the whole 4x6 grid, have students place timbre balls (3 of each) throughout the grid. Conduct by pointing to each chamber in succession to the steady beat, while class tries to perform the different timbres as they appear.

Try reciting the poem on top...

Try conducting a different path through the grid. You can rotate the grid and start at a new corner.

Can you find a path that ends with a basketball? A baseball?

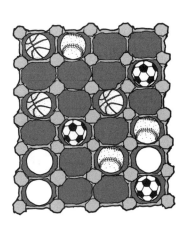

Creating a timbre score

Notice the four main repeating words of the text, and have the class choose a timbre to match each word. Then have students try to place the timbre ball into the correct place in the "score":

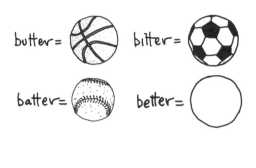

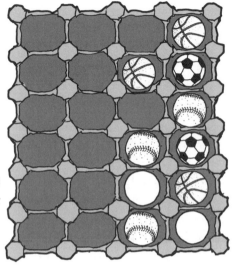

Following the timbre score, perform the first half of the poem, sounding the four timbres for the four repeating words.

Composing a melody for the rhyme

I have found this to be a very effective way for a group to compose a melody for a rhyme. It's a flexible, visual system that supports responding to and building upon each others' melodic ideas. For this work, you'll need six egg trays.

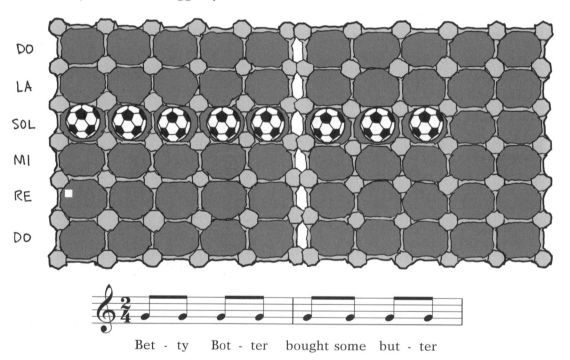

Bet - ty   Bot - ter   bought some   but - ter

First phrase

The egg tray uses one axis to show pitch, and the other to show rhythm. Sing the pentatonic scale from low Do to high Do and show where each pitch falls.

Start with a simple melody for the first phrase (every syllable on Sol):

Next, expand to a two-note melody. Ask kids to come up with a solution using Sol and Mi. You can either have kids sing their solution and you move the markers, or you could have a student move the markers and then sing from the notation.

Here's one example:

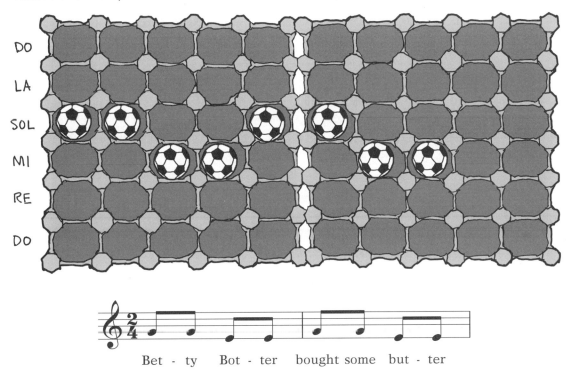

Bet - ty   Bot - ter   bought some   but - ter

Three notes

Adding La to the set of pitches will make for many more possibilities. With luck, several students will have different ideas, and you will be able to try them out and agree on the best one.

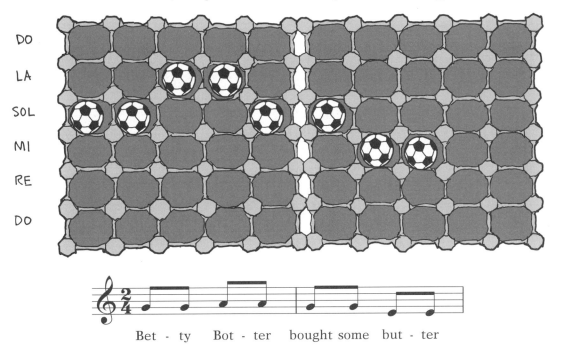

Bet - ty   Bot - ter   bought some   but - ter

Second phrase

To compose the second phrase, add two more egg trays and another set of 8 balls to represent the continuing text "…but, she said, this but-ter's bit-ter!"

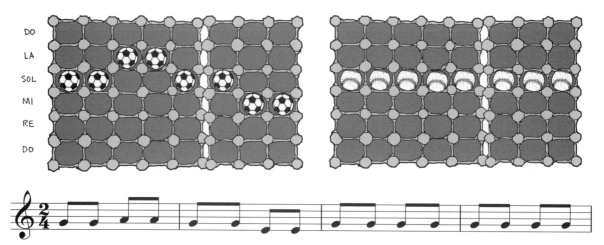

Invite solutions that use the notes of the scale that haven't been used. Here's one example:

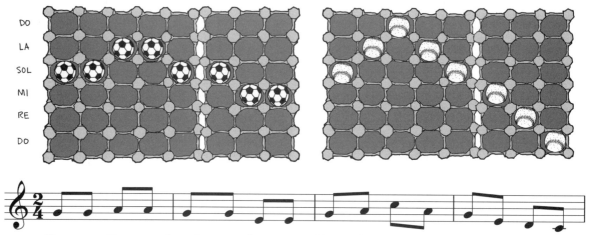

While it's possible that a solution will be reached immediately, it's more likely that one student will start with an idea that generates some discussion or reaction from the class. If your students are like mine, someone will try something that is really awkward to sing, such as:

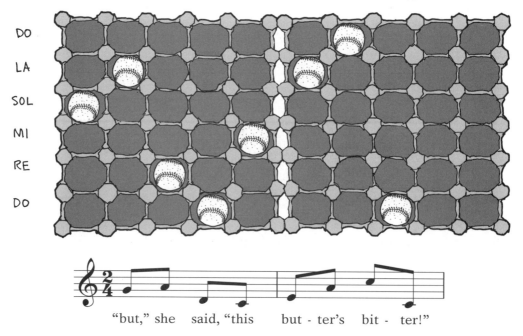

This is a great opportunity to notice what makes a melody hard to sing and what makes it easier. The octave jump at the end is strong, and we might want to save that but change the preceding notes.

Working with the arrangement
The arrangement at the end of this activity is not a score to teach your students but rather an example of the kind of results that might occur during the process described below.

Learning the melody
Have students learn the melody that the class composed. Some steps might be:
- Sing melody in solfege
- Translate melody into letter names
- Echo solfege patterns at instruments (orienting to the scale)
- Divide and conquer:
    - Teacher sings first phrase, students play second phrase. Switch.
    - Metals play first phrase, woods play second phrase. Switch.
    - Everyone plays entire melody.

Compose a special ending
Since the poem is long, it's good to have some melodic variety at the end of the song to wake the students up. You could go back to the egg cartons, or have individual students find a special ending and play their solution for the class.

Add the timbre accents
Have each section (glockenspiels, basses, xylophones, metallophones, drums, un-pitched percussion) huddle and decide on one repeating word in the text that will be their accent word. This could be the four major repeating words (butter, bitter, batter and better) or it might be a small word, like "the" or a seldom repeated word like "Betty." Have them decide on what sound they will make when they play their accent word. This could range from specific notes on their instrument to a glissando, clicking mallets…

Have one section perform the melody, while the other sections perform their accents. Next have a different section perform the melody. Have the students decide which version they like best. After trying out all the versions, see if the students have perceived which section is performing which accent words in the text.

Can you figure out which words are being accented by which instruments in the following score ?

Betty Botter

(Answers: drums = Betty Botter, glockenspiels = butter, bass xylophone = bitter, small percussion = "it" rhymes, xylophone = better, metallophone = batter)

FORTUNE TELLERS/ROSES ARE RED

A versatile children's plaything contains many musical lessons.

Preparing the material

You will need two fortune tellers. The first will contain funny messages for the introductory part of the lesson. The second will contain musical fortunes (see following pages for some ideas)

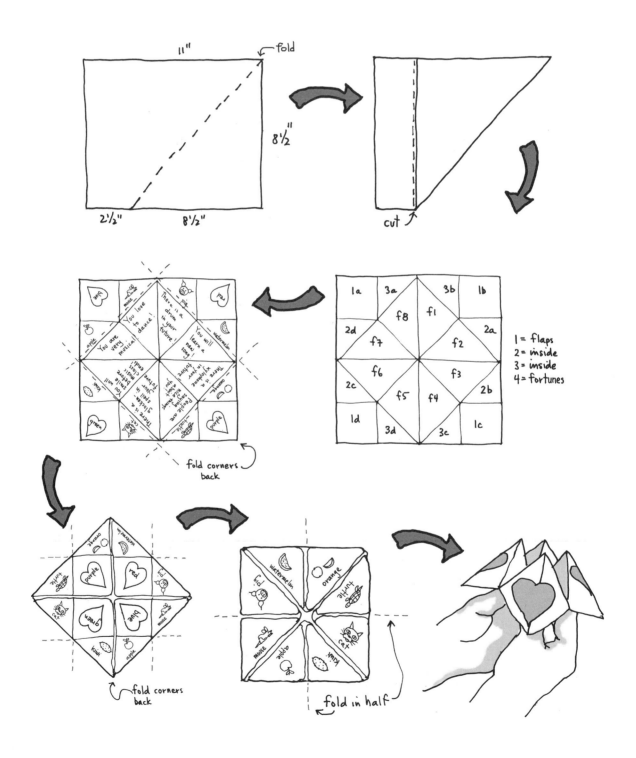

Categories

Fortune tellers are great for introducing rhythmic building blocks in categories. For mine, I picked colored hearts, fruit and animals as the three categories.

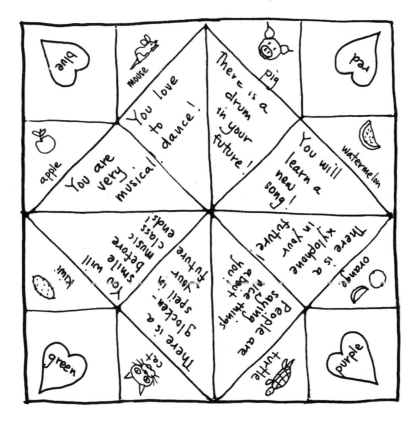

Fortune telling

Write funny fortunes in the blank triangles and invite students to have their fortunes told. This can be a fun way to start the class.

- Pick a color: R-E-D (fortune teller opens north/south, east/west, north/south)
- Pick a fruit: A-P-P-L-E (n/s, e/w, n/s, e/w, n/s)
- Pick an animal: Pig (unfold flap under the pig image and read fortune aloud): "You are very musical!"

Perform ostinati

Arrange words for complementary ostinati patterns.

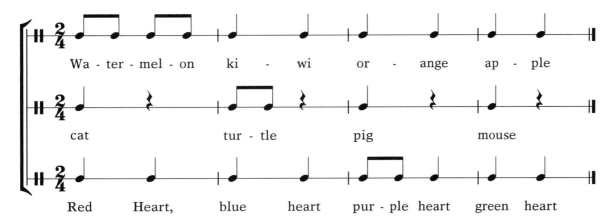

Introduce mystery poem

Have students try to guess the rhyme by looking at the rhythmic notation to the left. If everybody is stumped, add one word at a time until someone guesses the poem to the right:

Accompany rhyme with ostinati
Use the ostinati from the fortune teller to accompany the poem.

Partner game (learned from Doug Goodkin)
Stand back to back with a partner with each of you on either side of a line on the floor. Walk away from your partner for the first three lines of the poem. On "And so are you!" come back to your partner with both of your palms touching and freeze. Couples who move after the last line are eliminated. You could have them accompany the game on a drum until one pair becomes the winners.

Working with the arrangement
This is one possible pentatonic melody for this rhyme, that can be easily learned through singing, through solfege, and then discovered by the children on the instruments. Accompaniments and melodic ostinati could be invented by the children. I have invented some examples based on the word-list ostinati.

Musical fortunes
Return to the fortune teller, but this time with "musical fortunes" written inside the triangles. With children seated at the instrumentarium, choose a student and tell their fortune. The ensemble listens and accompanies the spelled words with improvisation in the pentatonic (or on bordun notes). The student receives her "musical fortune" and gets to do what it says as a solo. Then the full ensemble gets to give it a try.
- Play the scale from low to high
- Play the scale from high to low

- Play this rhythm on any notes: ta tate tate ta
- Play this rhythm on any notes: "watermelon orange purple heart cat"
- Sing the song while accompanying on C and G
- Play "Roses are Red" with your mallets backwards
- Play the melody with fingernails instead of mallets
- Sing the song and play your instrument in the rests
    etc.

Possible performance form

All students begin playing the partner game in front of the instruments. As groups are eliminated they take their place in the ensemble, building up the ostinati and then the melody.

    B-Section: Musical Fortune teller game (with a student conducting with the fortune teller)

    A- Section reprise- all play the song (this could be the last "musical fortune.")

Making fortune tellers with the students

At the end of this project the students will be eager to make their own fortune tellers, so have lots of square paper on hand... If you have some small stamp-pad images in categories, that can help with decorating, or students can draw free hand. You can display their fortune tellers on the wall for more rhythmic sequences before they take them home.

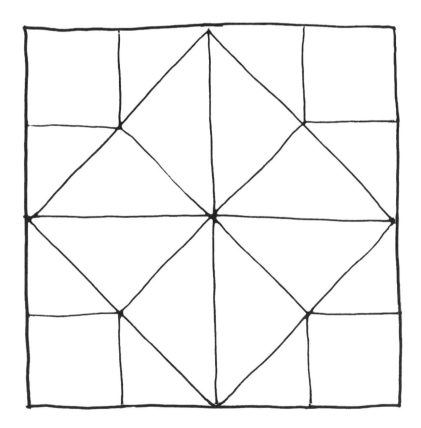

Roses are Red

Mother Goose   James Harding

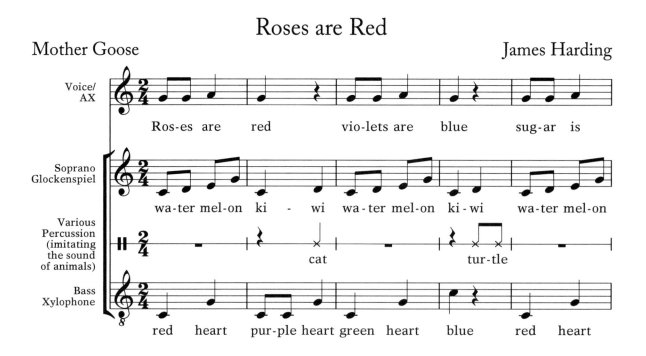

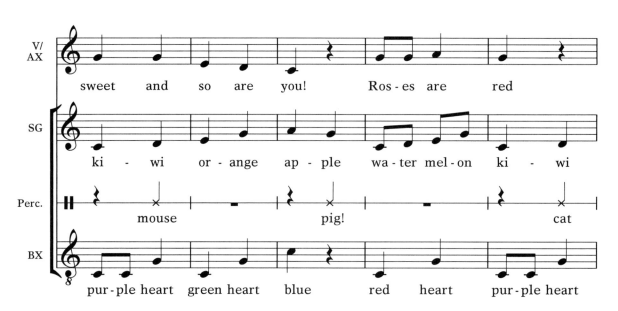

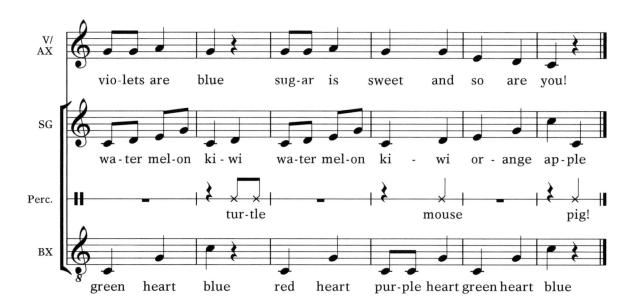

FEATURING THE ORFF ENSEMBLE

Working with the Orff Ensemble

Which Came First?

Loose Teeth

Gregory Griggs

Snakes and Ladders

Billy and Me

Mary, Mary, Quite Contrary

Modes of the Pentatonic Scale

The Wise Old Owl

Warm Hands, Warm

The Crooked Man

Dr. Seuss

Mrs. Hen

WORKING WITH THE ORFF ENSEMBLE

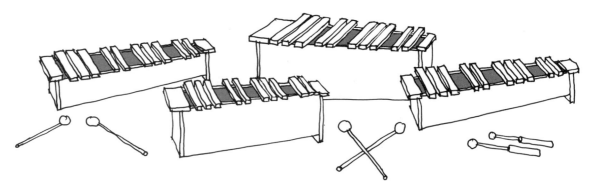

The activities that follow all lead to ensemble experiences on the Orff Instruments. If you are new to this ensemble, read Doug Goodkin's book "Play Sing and Dance" (Schott) to find out more about this remarkable educational invention, including information about its history, explanation of terminology, and detailed practical suggestions about how to use it with classes of young children. *

Much to explore without instruments

While I have aimed the lessons towards the ensemble experience, there are many ways of exploring these rhymes and poems without ever picking up mallets. I have started each lesson with several activities that can be explored without the instruments, followed by a suggested arrangement for the Orff ensemble and some notes about how to use the arrangement.

Below are a few important guidelines to keep in mind as you explore these lessons and my ensemble arrangements.

All children learn all parts

The arrangement examples in this book are meant to be fully understood by all of the players in the ensemble. The similar visual set up of each instrument makes it easy for a glockenspiel player to learn the bass xylophone part and vice-versa. A typical arrangement might include a melody, a melodic ostinato, an accompanying drone and a color part, and all these parts and the way they interact should be learned and understood by each student. Only later will specific instruments be assigned to specific roles in the ensemble (e.g. the basses playing the drone, the metallophones the melodic ostinato, the glockenspiels the color part and the xylophones the melody). Working in this way leads to a strong sense of musical ensemble within the group, where each child is aware of how her part fits into the whole.

Prepare students *before* they sit at an instrument

As much as possible, children should learn and internalize the musical patterns of an arrangement before they arrive at an instrument. Through speech ostinati, singing, and use of body percussion, all of the elements of an arrangement can be performed in ensemble before arriving at the instruments. Visual notation, solfege syllables and Curwen hand signs can be employed to clarify melodic patterns. With good preparation, a student can discover for herself how to play each part once she arrives at the instrument. In "Loose Tooth" children in the class form

---
* Doug Goodkin *Play, Sing & Dance* (London: Schott, 2002)

a pentatonic scale with their bodies, and melodies are learned from this visual pitch notation before going to the instruments:

do   re   mi   sol   la   do

Echo-location

It is often useful to help students connect pitch patterns to the instrument through echo practice (i.e. singing a melodic pattern using solfege syllables and having the students play back on the instruments). In all the examples in this book, "Do Re Mi" will be the same as "C D E" on the instruments

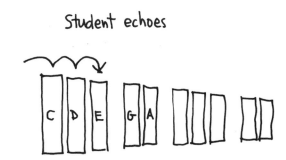

Divide and master

It is often useful to break down longer melodies into shorter sequences as part of the learning process, and the organization of the ensemble can facilitate this kind of approach. For instance, beginning with a two-part melody, a learning sequence could be as follows:

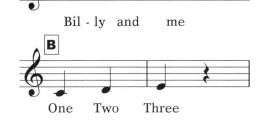

1. Teacher sings A, all Students play B
2. Students play A, Teacher plays B
3. Wood instruments play A, Metal plays B
4. Metal plays A, Wood plays B
5. All students play full melody AB

Playing technique

Part of the great attractiveness of these instruments is the relative ease of technique. Most young children will quickly learn how to produce a good sound with the mallets independently, but it is worth paying attention to the following:

Good   Too high   Too low

Posture

Set up instruments so that students can sit in a comfortable seated position (or standing) where the bars are about waist high (see illustration on previous page). The children should be able to hold their arms comfortably with elbows slightly bent and mallets extending naturally down in the line of the forearm. Bass xylophones and metallophones should have a short stool or chair, and glockenspiels should be placed on something to raise them up. Most of the rest of the range should be comfortable to play sitting cross-legged on the floor.

Mallet grip

Mallets should be gripped between thumb and the second joint of the first finger, with other fingers loosely curled around the handle. Watch out for children who are gripping too hard with their whole hand, or who are extending their pointer finger out onto the shaft of the mallet. Both of these techniques result in unnecessary tension and will make for a less fluid technique.

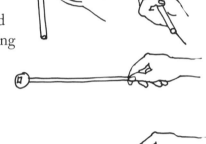

Striking

The mallet head should strike the center of the bar for the richest sound. In usual playing, the stroke should quickly bounce back off the bar, and not remain to dampen the sound. The image of pulling the sound out with the stroke (instead of pushing the sound in) usually is easy for children to understand.

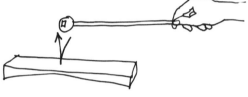

Playing with both hands

Many children need practice to incorporate their non-dominant hand, and will tend to pick out melodies and patterns with only one mallet. Consistent modelling the use of both mallets from the first lesson is worth the effort, and will help the children move towards a fluid technique. Body percussion patterns are wonderful ways to practice two-handed sticking (see "Patschen Exercises" in *Music for Children*, Volume I) *

Signals

You will want to have times where students are practicing or creating their own music on the instruments, and then you will want to be able to bring them back to focused attention. Audible or visible signals should be established for this purpose. Some examples:
- echo clapping sequence by teacher- students echo by clicking mallets.
- call and response- e.g. teacher "shave and a haircut" students "two bits!"
- audible signal: high trill on recorder by the teacher- students put mallets on head like antennae.
- physical shape: Teacher makes or calls out shape (e.g. "make a V"), students have to create it with their mallets.

* Carl Orff and Gunild Keetman *Music for Children* Volume I (London: Schott, 1958) p. 76

WHICH CAME FIRST?

The age old question. (Warning: this rhyme may lead to endless debates...)

Which came first,
The egg or the chicken?
Which came first,
The chicken or the egg?
The chicken's in the yard
But the egg's in the kitchen
Which came first,
The chicken or the egg?

Eggs and chickens
Can you clap Ta on every "egg"? Can you pat Ta-Te on every chic-ken? What sound or gesture could we make for "yard" and "kitchen?"

New variations
With a partner, invent your own sound gestures/movements for egg and chicken. If you want, make up other gestures for "yard" and "kitchen." Share your variation with the group.

Chicken/egg rhythms

Echo rhythms where egg = Ta and chick-en = Ta-Te:

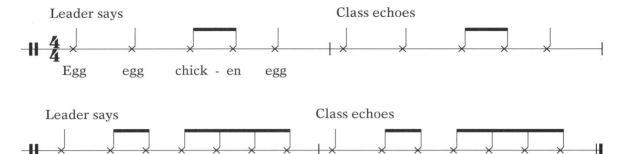

You can use this system in several activities, developing the skill of translating rhythmic speech to other kinds of rhythmic expression:

- Spoken rhythmic syllables (Ta Ta-te, etc.)
- Body percussion rhythm
- Un-pitched percussion
- Written rhythmic notation (place several patterns on the board and have the class match the written pattern with your spoken "egg/chicken" pattern.

Going in the opposite direction, you can clap a rhythm and have the class guess the words: "I went to a farm. The only things for sale were chickens and eggs. I bought four things. I'll clap the rhythm and you guess what I bought..."

Staccato and legato movement

With a partner, choose who will be the egg and who will be the chicken. Eggs move when the music is legato (smooth and connected, like the round, smooth shell of an egg). Chickens move when the music is staccato (short, clipped, like the movements of a chicken).

Can you make your movement match the quality of the music?

Teacher improvises staccato and legato music on a soprano recorder: e.g.

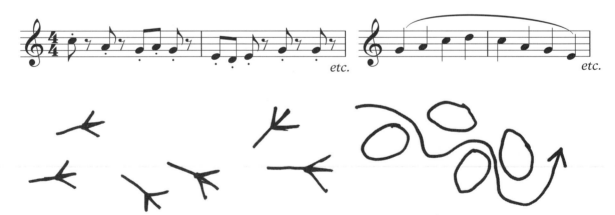

Working with the arrangement

Accompaniment to singing

This arrangement is mostly about accompanying a Do pentatonic melody with drones. The bass xylophone line is one example of a drone accompaniment. One basic arrangement could be to have students make up their own bordun accompaniments with egg/chicken rhythms that they create. For example: "Egg Egg Chicken Egg" could become any of the following:

Color parts

Assign higher instruments key words in the text, metals playing on "egg," woods playing on "chicken." You can add other colors (maybe un-pitched percussion instruments) for the repeating words "Which came first?" and the one-time words "yard" and "kitchen."

Melodic improvisation

Have two players trade question-and-answer improvisations, representing a dialogue between the chicken and the egg. The smooth egg can be played by a metallophone or glockenspiel, and the staccato chicken played by a soprano xylophone played with hard mallets.

Performance suggestion

Introduction

Argument between two opposing teams in rhythmic speech: "Chicken came first!" "Egg came first!" "Chicken Chicken Chicken Chicken" "Egg Egg Egg Egg" "Chicken Chicken" "Egg Egg" etc.

A section

Ensemble accompanies the singing of the song. Singers show motions for the key words.

Transition

Leader calls out various "egg chicken" rhythms, echoed by the ensemble either on their instruments or with clicking mallets or on separate, un-pitched percussion instruments.

B Section

Chicken and egg improvisations…dancers take turns dancing, with the idea that at the end of each phrase the dancer upstages her partner (a comic representation of the idea of coming first).

A section

Reprise

egg first   chicken first

Which Came First?

Music and Lyrics by
James Harding

which came first, the chick - en or the egg?

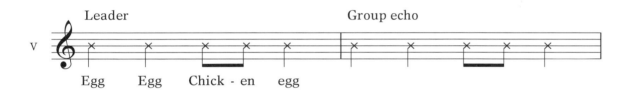

Leader   Group echo

Egg   Egg   Chick - en   egg

Egg   chick - en   chick - en   chick - en   *etc.*

LOOSE TEETH

A very vital theme for kids!

At The San Francisco School, first graders study food, shelter, and clothing and customs of people from all over the world, so I created this activity to stimulate interest in tooth traditions from many lands.

Wig-gle-y   wob-ble-y   al-most loose   Think I'm going to   lose this tooth!

Movement game: firm teeth/loose teeth

Students move in the space when teacher sings or plays the melody of the song. When the music stops, teacher indicates "firm" or "loose" (either with words or a musical signal) and students make shapes with their bodies, becoming firm or loose teeth.

Firm   **Loose**

- Test "firmness" of teeth by pushing gently… encourage students to use their muscles/balance to hold firm.
- Remind students that "loose" can still be balanced…can you wiggle your head, your arms, your knees, etc?
- Some teeth look firm but are really loose: experiment with creating a loose, still shape.
- With a partner, create a firm or loose shape.
- Students choose to be loose or firm; you guess which by testing them.
- Change movements: walk, run, skip, hop, jump, gallop, tip-toe, swing (teacher changes meter/tempo/dynamic of song to accompany):

Skipping and hopping and galloping:

Swinging:

The "dentatonic" scale (thanks to Peggy McCreary* for the pun)

Have children form rows of 8 firm teeth by the end of the song. Choose one group to stand facing the class:

Identify the solfege name of each tooth, and sing together up the scale. For a laugh, you can indicate each tooth by "flossing" the child with a soft maribou feather boa, or brush with a giant toothbrush...

Create a pentatonic scale by gently removing the "Fa" and "Ti" teeth:

Use this visual system to teach the melody, drone and color part in solfege (see score).

Tooth traditions from many cultures

While many North American children are told about the Tooth Fairy, there are many other tooth traditions. I found my students were fascinated to learn about tooth traditions from other parts of the world. Selby Beeler has collected many of them in her wonderful book *Throw Your Tooth on the Roof.*†

A few examples of tooth traditions:
- From Egypt: Children throw their tooth at the sun and say, "Bring me a new tooth." Smiles are bright because teeth come from the sun.
- From Cameroon: Chidren throw their tooth over the roof, shouting, "Take this bad tooth and bring me a new one." Then they hop around their house on one foot and everyone laughs.
- From aboriginal Australia: Children place the tooth inside the shoot of a plant (pandanus). As the plant grows, so will the new tooth.
- From Afghanistan: Children drop their tooth inside a mouse hole, saying, "Take my dirty old tooth and give me your small clean one instead."

Acting out tooth traditions

Have children create a skit with a partner or small group to show one of the tooth traditions.

---

* Peggy McCreary teaches Orff Schulwerk in Denver, Colorado
† Selby Beeter. *Throw Your Tooth on the Roof* (New York: Houghton Mifflin Harcourt, 2001)

Tooth tradition songs

When I explored this theme with 1st graders at The San Francisco School, we had adults from the community share their tooth traditions with us. One lovely and simple chant from Korea was taught to me by one of my colleagues, Yoon Hi Kim. Children who lose a tooth chant to a magic toad:

Korean Tooth Chant

Du - go - ba   Du - go - ba   Hunn - jyb   jül - ge   Sae - jyb   da - o

Translation: "Toad, Toad, I give you this old house, give me a new house"

Our visiting friend Kofi Gbolonyo[*] from Ghana taught our children about one tooth tradition from Ewe culture. When a child loses a tooth they must gather friends together. They throw the old tooth on the roof, and then dance seven times around the house, singing. There's a superstition that you must keep your mouth carefully covered if you lose a tooth, for if a lizard should see the hole in your mouth, your new tooth might not grow in.

Ewe (Ghana, Togo, Benin)
as learned from Dr. J.S. Kofi Gbolonyo

dza	dza	dza	'du - nye	tu	a -	du - nye	tu	a -
jah	*jah*	*jah*	*doo - nyeh*	*too*	*Ah*	*doo nyeh*	*too*	*Ah*

du - nye   tu   tsi   ne - dza   n'a   dua   na - to
doo nyeh   *too*   *Chee   neh   jah   nah   dwah nah   toh*

English Translation: "I've lost my tooth. Let rain fall so that the tooth may grow back."

---

[*] Dr. J.S. Kofi Gbolonyo is a professor of ethnomusicology at the University of British Colombia. His book of Ghanaian children's games will be published by Pentatonic Press.

Working with the arrangement

Preparing the instruments
Have children practice removing the bars from the instrument as if they were careful dentists, parents or teachers removing a loose tooth…. no yanking or twisting, please!

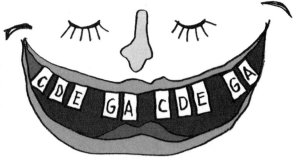

Prelude
Play up the scale, brushing each "tooth" with the mallets (tremolo) before moving on….at command "Rinse, please!" all play a glissando from high to low….

Melody
Review melody with solfege, and have children find it. Use visual reminder of "dentatonic scale" (see previous page)

Drone
Use this classic "broken drone" or have the children make up their own on C and G

Color part
Use this one, or have the children invent their own. This one cues on the end words "loose" and "tooth." Another color part could play after these words, on the rest. Other color parts could cue on the "wiggle-y, wobble-y" or on the words "loose" and "lose."

Possible form
Rondo with prelude. Episodes are "Tooth Tradition" Skits. Each time the rondo theme is played, add more elements: e.g. first time, singing only. Second time, melody and drone. Third time, add color part. Last time: Tutti!

Loose Tooth Song

James Harding

* Brushing teeth up the scale; conductor cues each move to the next tooth.

GREGORY GRIGGS

Wigs…now what could be more fun than that?
I thank Doug Goodkin for introducing me to this charming, indecisive
character.

Gregory Griggs, Gregory Griggs
Had twenty-seven different wigs
He wore them up, he wore them down
To please the people of the town
He wore them east, he wore them west
But he never could tell which he loved the best!

Intuiting the text
Have the students figure out the ending words using logic and their instinct for rhyme
Gregory Griggs, Gregory Griggs
Had twenty-seven different _____? (pigs? figs? gigs?)
He wore them up, he wore them _____
To please the people of the _____
He wore them east, he wore them _____
But he never could tell which he loved the _____

The pentatonic neighborhood:

Gregory has done so well at his wig shop that now he has two houses in town. When he strolls through the town he ends up at either one or the other. This is a nice visual set-up for singing in the pentatonic, for teaching the melody of the song, and for introducing the idea of melodic question and answer ending on the home note. Gregory's "houses" could be up on the wall or could be pads on the floor where conductors could actually walk and lead melodies with their feet.

Game 1: pentatonic walk
One student takes a walk through the scale, and the group sings the solfege.
Variation: Group watches the walk in silence, then sings what they saw.

Game 2: question and answer
One student walks a melodic question starting from the home tone Do, but not ending there. A second student walks a melodic answer starting from where the other student left off and bringing us back to the home tone.

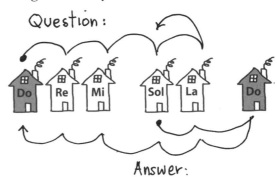

Do re mi sol la sol · sol la do la sol mi re do

Rhythms from wigs

Have students design and draw wigs for Gregory and then name and label them.

Game: Gregory's indecision

Set up the wig pictures in a gallery. One student is Gregory, and the class echoes the rhythm of what he says, either with words, body-percussion, or un-pitched percussion. When Gregory is finished, he says "I like the rest" and the group counts four rests and all play the tag "But he never can tell which he loves the best" to get back to the song…

Movement from wigs

Wigs have movement qualities, for example:

pathway: curly, straight, zig-zag

shape: spikey, rounded

energy: wild, limp, frizzy

Game: guess which wig? Have students make up a movement sequence combining two wigs. Class has to guess which wigs were the inspiration.

Variation: Accompany movements with vocal sounds or un-pitched percussion.

Gregory Griggs in the Orff Ensemble

Teaching the cadence

I like to start with the ending on this one. I have students practice clapping the rhythm of the last line of the poem "But he never could tell which he loved the best!" Try patting the rhythm with alternating hand technique:

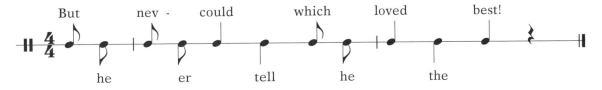

Try it on your knee. Try it with alternating fingers on your nose (good preparation for playing on a small glockenspiel bar)… When at an instrument, try playing it on one bar. Eventually lead group to the melody as written (if they don't discover it on their own).

Color parts

Play bordun notes high and low on "Up" and "Down." Can you still jump in on the ending?

First phrase

Make up a bordun to accompany the first phrase of the song "Gregory Griggs, Gregory Griggs, had twenty-seven different wigs." Repeat…subito piano…shhhhh!

Melody

The xylophone part for "He wore them up, he wore them down" is a classic crossover pattern. Which mallet stays on one note and which mallet crosses over?

Performance possibilities

Dramatic introduction

Drumroll... "Ladies and Gentlemen, we now present this year's Gregory Griggs Wig Collection..."

A Section: As ensemble plays arrangement, Gregory enters with wigs (could be children carrying the pictures of the wigs, wearing home-made wigs, etc.—a fashion show!)

B section: Gregory's Indecision (see previous page)

C Section: Gregory around the town: Melodic question and answer improvisation with the idea of home note.

A Section reprise: wigs parade off

But he never could tell which one he loved the best!

Gregory Griggs

Mother Goose   James Harding

SNAKES AND LADDERS

Known here as "Chutes and Ladders," this early board game was played in India
500 years ago

Snakes and ladders
Ladders and snakes
How will I ever win this race?
Ladders help me
Snakes are sliding down
Climb the ladder, reach the crown!

Playing with the text

Just as with "Which Came First?" this text contains two words that occur irregularly thoughout.
Recite or sing the text and have the children create and perform a gesture for "Snakes" and a
gesture for "Ladders."

Melodic motifs—climbing and falling

Teach two melodic motifs which appear in the melody:

Create combinations of the two symbols for students to read:

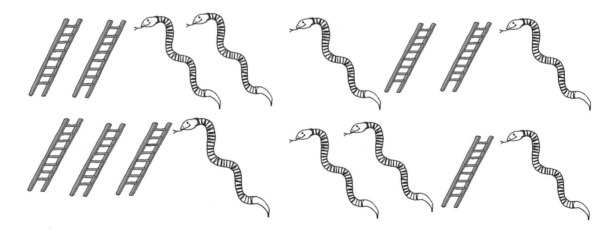

Variations

- Sing a combination and have the students guess. Sing with solfege. Play on recorder.
- Have a student or small group choose one combination and perform it for the class.
  Class has to guess the pattern.

Exploring rising and falling pitch patterns

Create images of ladders and snakes to represent rising and falling melodic patterns of 3, 4 and 5 notes in the pentatonic scale. Ladders start on Do and snakes end on Do.

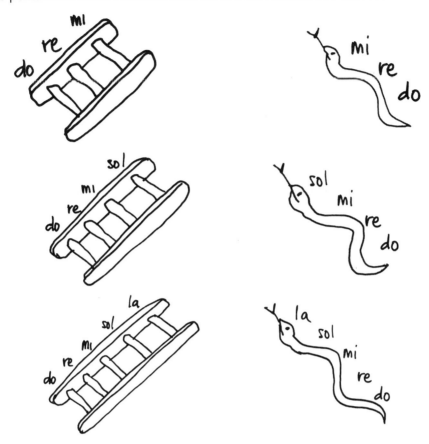

Playing with patterns

If you put the snakes and ladders images on cards, you can shuffle and deal cards out to students and have them create longer melodic patterns with them. These can be sung as episodes in a rondo form with the song "Snakes and Ladders" as the theme.

Board game score

You can create a snakes and ladders board game with the class by drawing a 6 by 6 grid and placing snakes and ladders that connect two squares. Players roll dice and move tokens that number of squares. If you land on the bottom of a ladder, you rise to the top; if you land on the head of a snake, you slide to the bottom.

You can make this a singing and pitch perception game by labelling the rows Do, Re, Mi, So, La and Do.

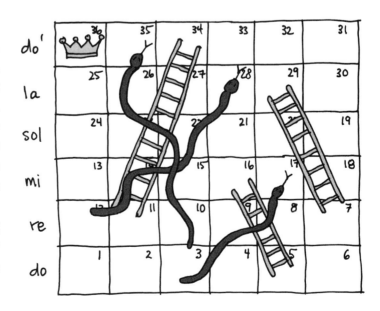

Working with the score

Teaching melody

The 6 by 6 grid is an excellent visual system for teaching melody. Use markers in each square to show the pitches. One marker = quarter note, two markers = eighth-note couplet. The example to the right shows "How will I e-ver"

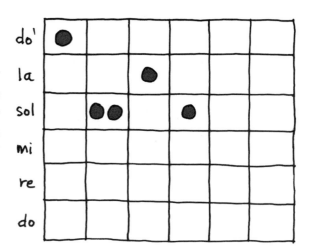

Technique practice: melodic ostinato

The motif is good for practicing the technique of alternating mallets on the barred instruments. Ask the students to practice "climbing the ladder" hand-over-hand, and then sliding back down the same way. You can have students play the combinations of snakes and ladders shown on the first page.

Practice the melodic ostinato as a canon with itself, with the second voice entering after the second beat:

Practice playing the ostinato with the melody, having some students sing the melody and the others play the ostinato as written in the score.

Un-pitched percussion color parts

The two un-pitched percussion parts in the score are each accenting a different repeated word in the main text. Maracas are accenting the snakes and the temple blocks are illustrating the ladders. Any other instruments could be used instead.

Possible performance form

Use song as a rondo theme, with episodes made up of melodic compositions using the snake and ladder solfege cards.

Snakes and Ladders

James Harding

snakes are slid - ing down   climb the lad - der,

reach   the   crown!

BILLY AND ME

I was attracted to this rhyme by the strange, polite line "How kind you be!" It's an example of the subjunctive, not used much in modern American English. Politeness and elegance can inspire humor (and sensitive ensemble playing, too).

Billy and Me
One, two, three
I love coffee and Billy loves tea
How kind you be!
One, two, three
I love coffee and Billy loves tea.

Play with phrase structure

This rhyme has the common phrase pattern of short, short, long. Here are some activities to draw attention to this form.

    Game 1: clap on the rests. Teacher says the poem and class has to listen for rests and fill them with a clap. Watch out—don't clap on "and!" Which phrases are short? Which phrases are long?

    Game 2: move, clap and turn. Move in a straight line on each phrase. Clap and turn sharply to face a different direction on the rests.

    Variation: end where you start. Try to return to your starting spot without making any curves in your pathway. Draw a diagram of your pathway. Try starting back to back with a partner or small group.

    Extension: Use strips of paper to create a diagram of a possible route, where the length of the strips match the lengths of the phrases. Can you dance the pathway that you created? Work with a partner: one creates the map, the other tries to dance it. Switch….

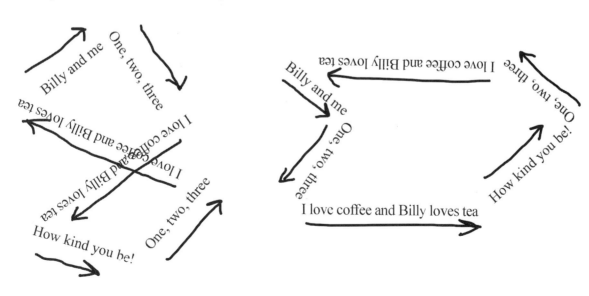

Coffee and tea items

Place real coffee and tea items out in view and review their names. Real objects are always more interesting to children than pictures (a trip to your local thrift shop might be in order).

Mug	Teaspoon	Cream pitcher	Sugar bowl	Cup and Saucer
Cream, scone, plate	Teapot, teacup, tea-bag	Tea strainer, tea kettle	Coffee pot, coffee cake	Coffee grinder, coffee filter

Composing ostinati with coffee and tea items

Guess the ostinato. Clap the rhythm of an ostinato made of two tea and coffee items. Have children guess which items you used. Variation: write the rhythmic notation of such an ostinato and have children figure out the items.

Children make their own ostinati to accompany the rhyme. Following the example above, students compose their own ostinati from the names of coffee and tea items. Use these ostinati as an accompaniment to the chant. Variation: Transfer ostinati to body percussion, un-pitched percussion instruments, or invented instruments. You can have kids explore the sound potential of the tea items...(but not on your best china!!!)

Tea skits

Polite behavior: Have children create skits showing what not to do at a formal tea party...according to Polite Paula. Or the very popular camp skit where one child is the narrator and the other stands behind her and puts her arms through the narrator's sleeves. Use the song Billy and Me as the rondo theme....

Boiling water: What happens to the molecules as water heats up? More and more rapid movement until they start to move so fast they separate and move away as water vapor. Perform "Tempest in a Teapot" showing a full kettle heating and cooling. You can accompany with vocal sounds—don't forget the kettle's whistle!

Billy and Me with the Orff ensemble

Melody

This melody has a logic to it for easy teaching.

- Identify pattern: sing melody to students and have them listen for patterns in the pitches
- Divide to learn: teacher/student (students sing "Do, Re, Mi" and "Mi, Re, Do" lines, teacher sings 'Sol-La" lines, switch). Other divides: wood/metal, solo/tutti, coffee lovers/tea lovers…

Bordun accompaniment

Have students create their own bordun accompaniments from their coffee and tea ostinati, or use the cross-over one from the score ("Tea and coffee").

Melodic ostinati

I created these two melodic ostinati (Sop. xy and alto met.) inspired by polite expressions. You can draw out the language from the kids by presenting them with tea party predicaments:

ASK POLITE PAULA

DEAR POLITE PAULA:
I'm at a formal tea party and I want to put cream in my tea but the cream pitcher is on the other side of my neighbor, the Duchess. I don't want to reach out across her and grab it…what should I do?
--Tea Party Perplexed

DEAR TEA PARTY PER-PLEXED:
Use your words…."Would you be so kind as to pass the cream?" should work nicely. Let's hope she's not hard of hearing, the poor Duchess!
-- Polite Paula

DEAR POLITE PAULA:
I'm asked to serve the Duchess her tea, and I don't know how much sugar she takes. I don't want to put in too much or too little. Should I just take a guess and hope for the best?
--Sugar Bowl Sufferer

DEAR SUGAR BOWL SUFFERER:
Again, a simple question will avoid countless possible embarrassing errors. If your sugar comes in lumps or cubes, simply ask the Duchess "One lump or two?" If she was counting on more than two, you will be gently setting a suggested limit
-- Polite Paula

Teaching melodic ostinati

For "Would you be so kind as to pass the cream?" have students practice playing the whole phrase on G, alternating mallets. Then change the last two notes to A and C. For "One lump or two" have children click mallets in the rests, "one lump" click "or two" click click.

Some performance suggestions

If you have a big group, let some dance, some play. Dancers choreograph a "tea dance" inspired by the phrase structure of the song (see previous page). Clink mugs and spoons to show the turns.

Boiling kettle introduction

Start from stillness and silence , like the cold water in the kettle. As water heats up, players add more and more agitated sound (any notes in the pentatonic), until kettle whistle blows (high recorder glissando) and then settle down after the kettle is taken off the stove. Then layer in the ostinati….

Boiling coda

After the melody has been sung and played sufficiently, give a signal for the students to start boiling again, in this case gradually altering their ostinati parts and making them more and more kinetic until full boiling occurs again…whistle, pour, sit down on a comfy seat (all players play "C" to the sitting-down cue).

Billy and Me

Mother Goose   James Harding

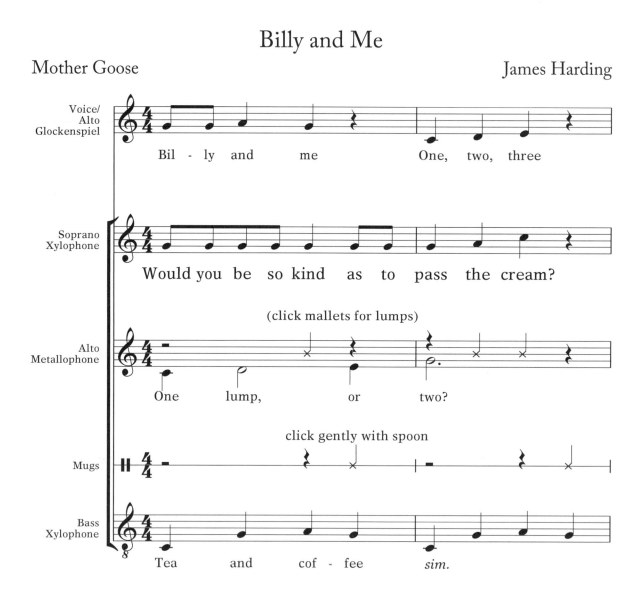

I love cof-fee and   Bil-ly loves tea   How kind you be!

One, two, three   I   love   cof-fee and   Bil-ly loves tea

MARY, MARY, QUITE CONTRARY

Once I realized that "contrary" meant "difficult" I had a whole new take on Mary's character. We are asking her a well-meaning question, "How does your garden grow?" and she's giving us a nonsense response. She's got an attitude! The idea of opposites is a rich theme to explore with children, and a great way to engage their musical minds.

Mary, Mary
Quite contrary
How does your garden grow?

With silver bells
And cockleshells
And pretty maids all in a row!

Playing with opposites

Musical Opposites: Dividing the poem into question and answer, play with expressive opposites in as many musical categories as you can.

Question/answer game with opposites: Students are Mary (who, as we know, is always quite contrary). For example, if teacher reads the question in a high voice, the students answer in a low voice.

Teacher: Slow/Students: fast Teacher: Soft/Students: LOUD! etc.

Chart of musical opposites: Making a chart of musical opposites is a great way to review musical vocabulary. Here's an example of a table of musical opposites by element:

Pitch	Tempo	Dynamic	Rhythm	Articulation	Emotion
high/low, rising/falling	fast/slow, accelerando/ralentando	loud/soft, crescendo/diminuendo	straight/swing	staccato/legato	friendly/mean, happy/sad

Guessing Game: Students (individual or small group) perform both parts of rhyme using opposites, and class has to guess which opposites they are using. The students could choose opposite pairs from the chart, or you could write opposite pairs on cards for them to pick.

Contrary solfege

If Mary's teacher sings "Do-Re-Mi" guess what she sings? "Mi-Re-Do." Try many short patterns in the pentatonic. Watch out—this can be habit-forming!

Leader	Class	Leader	Class	Leader	Class
do re mi	mi re do	do do re mi	mi mi re do	do do sol	sol sol do

Movement opposites

This rhyme is a good opportunity to explore opposites in movement.

Direction	Space	Relationship	Shape	Pathway
up/down, left/right, forward, backward	Moving/staying in one place, low/high	close/farapart	big/small, low/tall	curving/straight

Reaction game: perform rhyme (either vocally or instrumentally) to accompany students as they move, switching between opposites on question and answer.

Plants in Mary's garden

What the nose knows: investigating plants through smell. Many youngsters today have very little contact with or knowledge of living plants. For this exercise I bring in five live aromatic herbs unlabeled so the students can try to identify them through smell and touch. I give each group a time limit for investigating each plant and I sing the melody "Mary, Mary" (see following score) as a signal to pass the plants on. After everyone has investigated all the plants, I give the name of each one and ask them what they know about these herbs.

Some common aromatic plants categorized by the rhythm of their names:

Mint (♩)	Basil (♫)	Rosemary (♫♪)	Lemon Balm (♫♩)	Pennyroyal (♬♫)
Thyme, Sage, Dill	Spearmint, Fennel	Horseradish	Lavender, Lemongrass	Coriander, Echinacea

Composing ostinati with plant names

For the purposes of rhythmic ostinato building, you need plants with names that represent the 5 building blocks (see chart above).

Two plant ostinati: Have students create a rhythmic ostinato using the names of two plants. For example, "rosemary basil."
- **Game 1** Clap the rhythm of your ostinato and have the class guess which two plants you used.
- **Game 2** All students clap the rhythm of their own ostinato and try to find someone who has the same rhythm.

Four beat ostinato with fragrant rest: Have students create a four beat ostinato using up to three plant names. One beat has to be a rest, which can be represented by an inhalation:

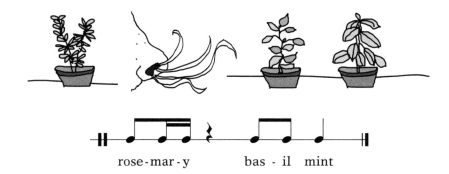

rose-mar-y   bas - il   mint

Working with the arrangement
As with all of these arrangements, you can keep it as simple as you want.

Simplest: sing melody with bordun accompaniment.

More input from students: Students make up their own bordun accompaniments using their plant ostinato rhythms.

Add color parts (make up your own, but try these too):
- Clusters on "Mary, Mary" and "trary"expressing her character. Play any two adjacent bars on these syllables
- Glockenspiels play drone notes on "bells" and "shells"
- Alto metallophone illustrates "grow" and then "in a row"

Melody: Have some motivated students learn the melody. "With silver bells" is a nice place to start.

Other performance ideas
Introduction: Perform question and answer game of opposites as a spoken prelude to the performance. Act out the dialogue as a skit…find a grumpy Mary!

B Section: opposite shapes
Have students work with partners to express pairs of opposites with their bodies: near/far, together/separate, wide/narrow, twisty/straight, big/small, high/low, growing/shrinking, rising/falling, tight/loose. Perform your opposites in time with the ostinato chant, "How does your garden grow?"

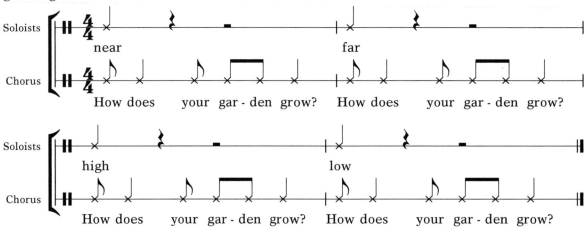

Coda
Have drone continue and perform contrary motion question and answer ending with the cadence "Sol Sol Do"…(see previous)

Other opposites resources
Book: *I'm Quick as a Cricket* by Brian and Audrey Wood. A wonderful book of animal opposites: "I'm lazy as a lizard, busy as a bee, put it all together and you have me!" *

---

* Brian and Audrey Wood, *I'm Quick as a Cricket* (New York: Child's Play Intl. Ltd., 1998) p. 20

Mary Mary Quite Contrary

Mother Goose

James Harding

Mar - y Mar - y quite con-trar - y   How does your gar-den grow? With

sil - ver bells and cock-le shells and pret-ty maids all in a row

Coda

MODES OF THE PENTATONIC SCALE

Same notes, different home tone

Up to this point, all arrangements have been set in the C pentatonic scale wherein Do (C) is the home tone, and the drone is comprised of C and G (Do and Sol):

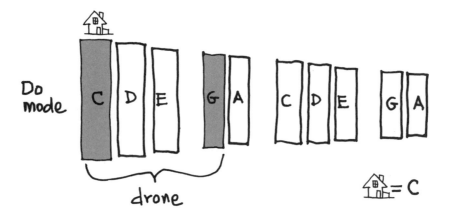

The arrangements in the following section also use the C pentatonic scale, but the home note is no longer C. Now it is Re, Mi or La, the syllables we use to give these modes their name. This means, of course, that the accompanying drone will also change.

"The Wise Old Owl" is in the Re mode, therefore D is the home tone:

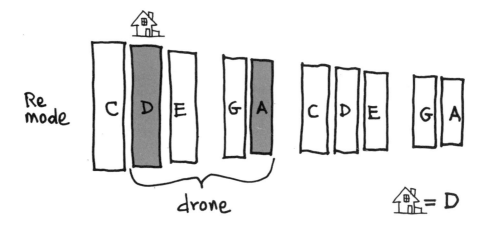

"Warm Hands, Warm" is set in the Mi mode, therefore E is the home tone. (Note that the drone is now an octave, because there is no fifth to play):

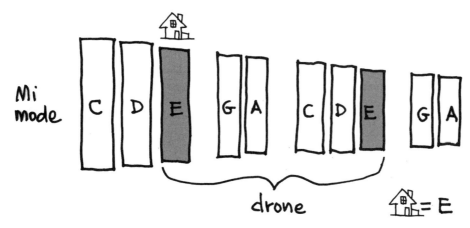

"The Crooked Man" and "Dr. Seuss" feature the La mode, therefore A is the home tone, and the drone is played on A and E:

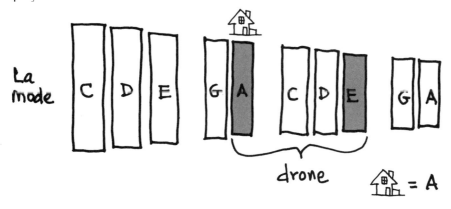

Why modes?

These modes of the scale bring with them a welcome variety of moods. Just as composers use minor and major keys to convey different emotions, so we can use the Re, Mi and La modes of the pentatonic to set poems or rhymes with a more introspective feeling. I find that children quickly grasp the new "rules" of the modes, it's simply a matter of finding the new home note and new drone notes. However, at The San Francisco School we usually wait until 2nd grade to introduce these modes, after plenty of experience with the Do mode of the scale.

Two modes at once

The last example "Mrs. Hen" features a setting that changes back and forth between the La and Do modes of the scale. This is essentially a pentatonic melody harmonized by two chords, the I chord (C major) and the vi chord (A minor). In the B section of the setting, the students get a taste of improvising over each chord by playing in ranges of the scale:

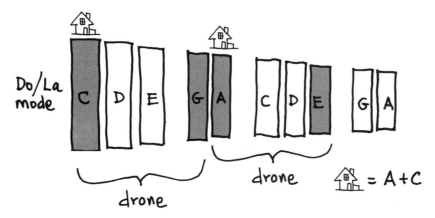

THE WISE, OLD OWL

This is a wonderful poem about the value of listening. The many repeated words in the text make an interesting pattern to explore. The nocturnal world of the owl is supported by the mysterious sounding Re mode of the pentatonic scale.

A wise, old Owl sat in an oak
The more she heard, the less she spoke
The less she spoke, the more she heard
Couldn't we be more like that wise, old bird?

Playing with word repetition in the text
Attention game: Gestures for repeating words: Have students find repeating words in the poem. As a class, create gestures to accompany each of the main repeating words in the poem…(or learn the ASL signs below). Add gestures gradually so the group has time to practice.

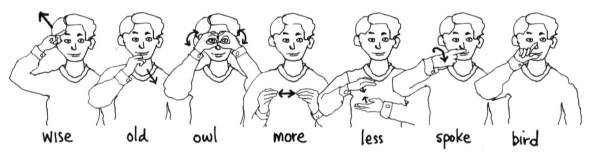

wise   old   owl   more   less   spoke   bird

As a class, decide how to treat the non-repeating words "owl", "oak", and "bird" (some classes want owl and bird to be the same gesture, others want two distinct gestures).

Recite poem aloud with gestures; silently with gestures.

Variation: Un-pitched percussion. With a visible array of un-pitched percussion have students imagine the instruments playing for each of the key words in the poem. What instrument might you choose to play "less" or "more"? One player, one sound for each word below.

wise   old   more   less   heard   spoke

- Recite poem aloud with instruments playing on key words.
- Recite poem silently with gestures and instruments .

Game: the owl in the forest
Children with hand percussion form a circle.
One child (the owl) stands in the center, blindfolded.
Owl declares which instrument she will be hunting for, e.g. the claves.
As the class sings or chants "The Wise Old Owl," instrument players
circle 'round while playing on their particular words.
At the end of the song, players freeze.
Owl tries to move towards and touch the player of her chosen instrument (a la blind man's bluff).

The less you speak the more you...
As more and more of the text is dropped, the more silence takes its place. This is a great exercise for internalizing the steady beat, and it lends itself to variations featuring movement.

```
Couldn't we be more like that wise, old bird?  ξ
Couldn't we be more like that wise, old    ξ    ξ
Couldn't we be more like that wise    ξ    ξ    ξ
Couldn't we be more like that    ξ    ξ    ξ    ξ
Couldn't we be more    ξ    ξ    ξ    ξ    ξ
Couldn't we be    ξ    ξ    ξ    ξ    ξ    ξ
Couldn't    ξ    ξ    ξ    ξ    ξ    ξ    ξ
    ξ    ξ    ξ    ξ    ξ    ξ    ξ    ξ
```

Some ways to work this:

- Say words, clap the rests (like BINGO)
- Clap words, silence on the rests
- Say words, hoot like an owl on the rests

- Move and say words, stop and clap rests in place.
- Say the words in place, move and clap on the rests.
- Substitute a hand drum or small percussion instrument for clapping.
- Half the class moves on the words and the other half moves on the rests.

Working with the arrangement

The pentatonic neighborhood revisited

Like Gregory Griggs, the owl has two houses in town—one up and one down (in fact, she's Gregory's neighbor). Her melody starts downtown and ends uptown. This is a nice visual system for learning a new home note in the scale. This scale is a mode of the pentatonic scale, called "C pentatonic, Re mode" (or "Re pentatonic on D"). It has a unique symmetry, and a somewhat haunting sound, well suited for introspective or mysterious moods.

Improvise a last line

On the line "Couldn't we be more like that wise, old bird?" have students improvise a melody that brings them from high "Re" to low "Re." Play the following game to hear the improvisation.

Solo/Tutti game: All students play melody (or bordun) while teacher walks around ensemble and chooses a soloist for the last line. At the last line, all stop and listen to the soloist. Repeat (teacher can indicate soloists, duets, trios, sections, or tutti).

Performance suggestion

A section: ensemble plays melody, accompanied by borduns. For last line, all improvise melodic phrase ending on the home-note.

B Section: basses continue playing bordun accompaniments. Two improvisers on wood and metal improvise freely in the re-pentatonic scale. Over this, the rest of the ensemble clicks the rhythm of "Couldn't we be more like that wise, old, bird?", following the diminishing pattern from the game. As more rests occur, the more the improvising instruments are revealed...

A section reprise...

Related to the theme of silence and listening

I used this arrangement for a dream sequence in a second grade play based on the book *The Loudest Noise in the World*.* In the story, the prince of the land of Hubbub wants to hear the loudest sound in the world, and sends messengers all over the kingdom so that everyone can shout "Happy Birthday" at the same time! In our play, one messenger returning home has a dream of the owl, and when she wakes up she decides that she will be able to hear the loudest sound just like the prince if she listens instead of shouting "Happy Birthday." She tells her friend about the idea....and she tells a friend....and so on....When the big count down comes "5....4....3...2....1.....
..........[silence]" The prince hears silence for the first time...and enjoys it!

In our owl scene, we used blacklight. We painted paddle-fans with glow-in-the-dark rhythmic symbols, with rests on the flip side. For the B section, the dancers flipped their fans to show more and more glowing rests....

See also Doug Goodkin's treatment: "The Owl" in *Intery Mintery* (Pentatonic Press).

---

* Benjamin Elkin, James Daugherty. *The Loudest Noise in the World.* (New York: Viking Press, 1954). Thanks to my friend Laura Burges, 3rd grade teacher at The San Francisco School, for introducing me to this wonderful story.

The Wise, Old Owl

Mother Goose

James Harding

WARM HANDS, WARM

An exploration of touch in the Mi mode

cold hands

Warm hands, warm!
The farmer's gone to plow
If you want to warm your hands
Warm your hands now!

warm heart

Warm hands to the beat

This is a rhyme about farmers plowing their fields in cold weather. What are some ways you can warm your hands? Can you make your hand-warming show the steady beat? Can you make a rhythmic ostinato with your hand-warming?

Some possibilities: rubbing hands together, tucking under arm-pits, blowing warm breath onto hands, putting on gloves or mittens...

Cold hands, warm heart!

Find the coldest hands in the room. Everyone start with a partner; at the end of the chant, touch palms with your partner. Whoever's hands are colder moves into the center to look for a new partner; whoever's hands are warmer forms a circle facing in. When the coldest handed person is discovered, he or she goes around and touches everyone's hands. This would be a good time to learn the ostinato:

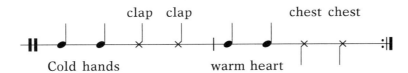

Half the class accompanies the rhyme with the ostinato. Switch.

Hand sculpture perception game (inspired by Barbara Haselbach*, Orff Institute)

In partners. One partner closes her eyes. While chanting the poem, the other partner makes an interesting shape using both of his hands and holds the shape still. At the end of the song, the partner with eyes closed feels the shape her partner made and then tries to reproduce it with her own hands. Once she thinks she's got it, she opens her eyes. The game should be repeated several times so that each partner gets a few turns to play both roles.

a hand sculpture to reproduce

---

* Barbara Haselbach is the author of many books, including *Improvisation, Dance, Movement* (MMB Music, 1981) and *Dance Education: Basic Principles and Models for Nursery and Primary School* (London: Schott, 1979). She is the director of the Orff Schulwerk Forum.

Variation with Curwen-Glover hand signs

In this variation, the partner with her eyes open receives a hand-shape idea from the teacher and then the partner with his eyes closed feels and copies the shape:

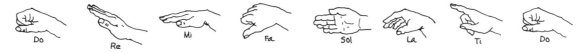

These hand signs are a kinaesthetic and visual notation system for pitch often used in conjuction with solfege in the Kodaly music education system. If the students are already familiar with them, this game could be a kind of review, where they guess the solfege syllable by feeling its shape in the hands of their partner. If they're unfamiliar with the signs, this game is a good introduction.

Other variations

Play game above with the ASL sign alphabet. You could have children spell words to each other with their hands.

Use Curwen-Glover hand signs to introduce melody

The melody is only four pitches, so it's a good candidate for teaching with the Curwen-Glover hand signs:

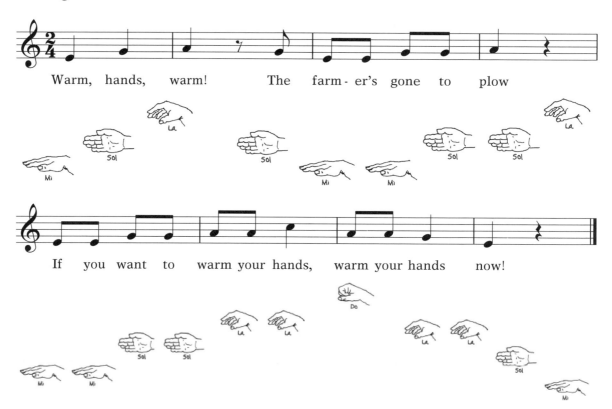

Graphic notation with hand prints

Have students create a visual composition using their hands dipped into washable paint (finger paint works well). Once these are dry, experiment with interpreting these visual patterns as music. How would you sing this? Play it on the recorder? Play it on the xylophone? Do you read the score from left to right, or does a conductor lead the group from place to place?

Temperature words and dynamic

Brainstorm a list of temperature words that could be used to describe hands (both hot and cold). Write these onto cards, shuffle, and draw out four. Have the class put them in order from hot to cold. Perform these as an echo, paying special attention to dynamic. The colder the hand the softer the dynamic of the echo.

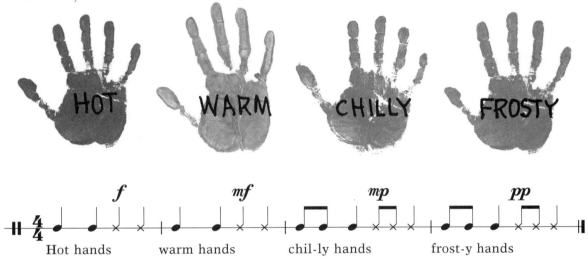

Variation with hand drums

Simple frame drums lend themselves both to rhythmic work and to movement. The exercise above emphasizes dynamic and is a good occasion for exploring variations in technique.

Have the drummers create a simple movement sequence with their drums for the song "Warm Hands, Warm."

Working with the arrangement

This setting is very spare, and the Mi pentatonic mode makes it sound mysterious or maybe even mournful. You can add to the frosty atmosphere with chime trees or other crystalline sounds. The melody can be sung as a canon and can also be played very easily on the soprano recorder. The glockenspiel outlines the mode. The bass part is an extension of the "Cold Hands/Warm Heart" accompaniment.

Ideas for performance:

Have a group of hand drum players/dancers. a group of recorder players/singers, and some Orff ensemble players.

Introduction

Hand print graphic score is displayed. While an E drone is played by a bass instrument, a conductor pulls sounds from the ensemble by pointing to various symbols. This can be a way of introducing the various timbre groups of drums, recorders and Orfff Instruments.

A section

The ostinati layer in (glock and bass xylophone parts). Song sung twice by hand drummers and recorder players. Recorders play melody 2x while hand drum players perform choreography.

B section

Recorder players speak the four temperature hands (e.g. "hot hands, warm hands, chilly hands, frosty hands") and the hand drum players echo.

A section

Back to the melody, this time performed in canon.

Coda

All performers join in whispering "Cold hands... warm heart..."

Warm, Hands, Warm!

Adaptation of English Rhyme
by James Harding

THE CROOKED MAN

Here's an ideal rhyme for exploring the fantastic world of tangrams, a
geometrical puzzle from China

There was a crooked man
Who walked a crooked mile
He found a crooked sixpence
Upon a crooked stile
He bought a crooked cat
Who caught a crooked mouse
And they all lived together in a little, crooked house

—Mother Goose

Shape game

Pass out slips of paper with the words "man" "mile" "sixpence" "stile" "cat" and "mouse." Ask
students to make a shape with their bodies when they hear their word mentioned in the poem
as you recite it. Everyone has to make her/his own shape for "house."

- Find other students with the same word to create group shapes
- Put the words/shapes in order
- Focus on the adjective: is your shape crooked? How can you make it crooked?
  What's another adjective we could use for a variation? (try "twisty" "wiggly" "tiny"
  "giant" "scary" "silly" etc.)
- Make a group shape for "house" that includes everyone

Tangrams

Give groups, partners or individual students a set of tangrams and a puzzle to solve:

Mile   Sixpence   Stile   Cat   Mouse

Can you rearrange the shapes to form another character from
the poem in the time it takes me to recite the rhyme?

The real tangrams puzzles only show the final silhouette
of the shape, which I found quite challenging for my second
graders, especially with a time limit!

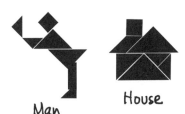

Man   House

Composing a crooked tune

My melodic setting of this poem came from a compositional process with second grade students.
Composing a melody as a group is a challenging activity, but I have discovered that using a flex-

ible visual system helps keep the process fluid and keeps everyone engaged. The grid below could be created on a white board with moveable magnetic circles for the pitch markers.

Start with a "straight" melody (monotone on Sol) and have students make the melody more "crooked" by moving tones. After a student makes a change, always sing back the transformed melody and have the class echo. Some principles of effective and easy to sing melodies that you will discover in this exercise are:

- Stepwise melodic motion is easier to sing.
- Jumps are exciting and possible to sing, but two jumps in a row are more awkward.
- It's elegant after jumping to move stepwise in the other direction.

Working with the arrangement

La pentatonic bordun

I constructed this arrangement around the melody that my second graders came up with (see above), adding a broken bordun on the contrabass bars on A and E to support the La-centered melody. Should your students create their own melody, you will need to devise a bordun that supports it. (The bass xylophone part is a more elaborate bordun for a special challenge.)

Review melody on the instruments

Have all students find the melodic motif on the instruments.

The motif is used for the first six lines of the poem, except for the two syllables of "six-pence."

Teach or compose ending phrase

I asked students to find a way of playing "And they all lived together in a little crooked house." on their instruments, and the melody in the score is a composite of ideas from several students. If you're teaching my arrangement, draw attention to the ascending patterns at "and they all" and "crooked house" with the connecting passage "lived to-geth-er in a lit-tle" as doubled notes descending.

Color part

Fill in the rests in the poem with a clap. Which line doesn't have a rest at the end?
Instead of clapping, play octave A's on your instrument. Woods play the melody and metals play the color part. Switch.

B section improvisation

Have soloists improvise melodically in the scale, echoing the rhythm of spoken phrases:

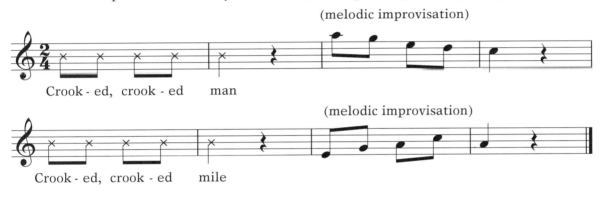

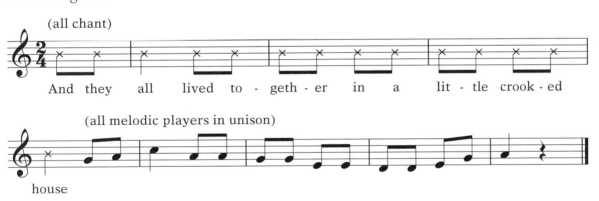

etc. leading to...

Extensions

Tangrams are a great material for animation. To see "The Crooked Man" as an animation project with 2nd graders from The San Francisco School, go to http://vimeo.com/15149518

The Crooked Man

Mother Goose

James Harding

and they all lived together
in a little crooked house!

DR. SEUSS

Inspired by his birthday (March 2nd), this exploration evolved into a drama and movement piece glorifying reading and the importance of being yourself.

Be who you are
Say what you feel
Those who mind don't matter
Those who matter don't mind!

—Theodore Giesel (aka Dr. Seuss) *

Speech piece with titles

Create a speech piece using titles of some of Dr. Seuss's most famous books. I chose four of my favorites to convey four complementary rhythms:

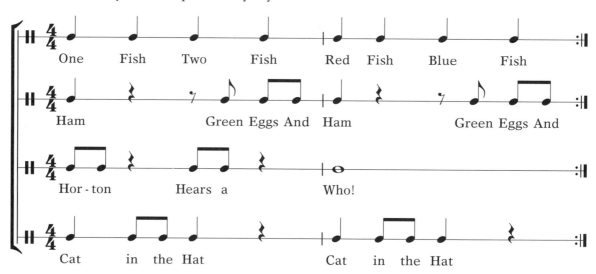

Other great titles for building ostinati:

    Fox in Sox, The Lorax, The Foot Book, Hunches in Bunches, There's a Wocket in my Pocket, Yertle the Turtle...

Transfer ostinati to body percussion or un-pitched percussion.

Conducting exercises

One conductor: Holds up book to bring in pattern; brings it down to stop.

More than one conductor: Each has book, starts pattern by opening book, stops by closing.

Develop signals using books for dynamic, articulation, timbre...

---

* This statement has been attributed to Theodore Giesel, but it's not clear when he said it. Another similar statement "I meant what I said and I said what I meant" comes from *Horton Hatches the Egg* (1940). "A person's a person no matter how small" comes from *Horton Hears a Who!* (1954). "From there to here, from here to there, funny things are everywhere," comes from *One Fish Two Fish Red Fish Blue Fish* (1960).

Working with the quotation

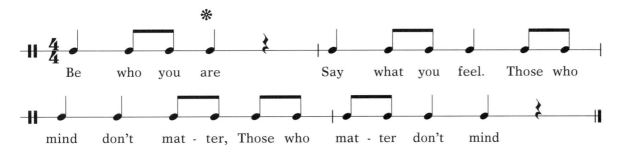

Be who you are   Say what you feel. Those who

mind don't mat-ter, Those who mat-ter don't mind

Discuss meaning (there's a lot to discuss!).

Have students find repeating words "mind" and "matter" and accompany with body percussion sounds.

Recite in canon.

Recite over other ostinati (see previous page).

Skit

Four seated actors, each reading a Dr. Seuss book.

Annoying Person enters asking questions like, "What are you reading?" and "What are you doing?" Readers improvise answers and then finally announce the title of their book, which activates the ostinato, which plays in the background of the next dialogue. Repeat until all ostinati are in. Annoying Person then recites the quotation "Be who you are..." to the audience to end the skit.

Choreography with books

Books can be an inspiring prop for movement exploration and choreography. I used the "One Fish Two Fish" melodic ostinato played on a bass xylophone to accompany my students' explorations.

Solo

- Book in hand...pathways in space
- Book balanced on head, shoulder, arm, back, etc.
- Opening and closing book
- Book in front of face/covering and revealing face

With partner or group

- Mirroring
- Shadowing
- Diamond formation shadowing
- Echoing movement phrase
- Passing books

Working with the arrangement

Composing a Melodic Ostinato Arrangement

I composed this melodic ostinato for "One Fish, Two Fish" which everyone learned:

One Fish, Two Fish,   Red Fish, Blue Fish

I then had students find melodic patterns for their favorite Dr. Seuss title from our speech piece. Opposite is the arrangement that I settled on, choosing the patterns that I thought worked best together.

Compose melody

The ostinati are in La Pentatonic on A. After the ostinati have been composed, ask students to come up with a melody for the quotation "Be who you are..." with the home note La.

Ensemble work

The challenge of playing in a layered ostinati ensemble is to keep your own part while hearing how it fits in to the whole. Try building up to all parts at the same time by trying out combinations:

- Cat in the Hat/One Fish Two Fish,
- Horton Hears a Who/Cat in the Hat, etc.
- Then combinations of three ostinati, then four.

A possible performance form

Book dances performed with ostinati accompaniment; after each dance, students sit down to read.

Skit: Annoying Person comes in, improvised dialogue, ostinati re-activated leading to quotation.

Quotation: Sung, sung as canon, danced as canon (with simple book choreography).

Honoring other authors

Look up the birthdays of other popular children's book authors and celebrate them by creating a similar composition built from their famous titles:

A.A. Milne (January 18th), Maurice Sendak (June 10th), Beatrix Potter (July 28th), JK Rowling (July 31st), Roald Dahl (September 13th), William Steig (November 14th)...

Dr. Seuss

James Harding
with melodic ostinati composed by
2nd Grade Students

MRS. HEN

This rhyme caught my eye and ear because I couldn't make it easily fit into a standard meter. My solution was to mix up the meter but keep an ongoing, steady pulse throughout. There is a great deal of exploration to be done with this miniature scene…

Chook! Chook! Chook! Chook! Chook!
Good Morning, Mrs. Hen!
How many chickens have you got?
Madame, I've got ten:
Four of them are yellow
Four of them are brown
Two of them are speckled red,
The finest in the town!

Dramatic reading

Questions to pose to the class: How many characters are in the rhyme? Who are they? Who's making the sound of the chooks? Who is Madame? There are no right answers, of course, but it's fun to ask the children to come up with theories…

Three vocal timbres: If the "chooks" were the baby chickens, try performing the poem with three distinct timbres: one for the chickens, one for Madame, and one for Mrs. Hen. You could also divide the class to represent the three timbres/characters.

Dramatic timbres: What if Madame is a kind, old woman? What if Madame is a sly fox wanting to eat the little chickens? Have individual students volunteer to perform solo with their three character voices.

Un-pitched percussion dialogue

Sitting in the circle, have three un-pitched percussion instruments selected for performing the first four lines of the poem: one sound for the chickens, one for "Madame," and one for Mrs. Hen. Perform the dialogue with these instruments, and then use the last four lines of the poem as a signal to pass the instrument to the person to the right, who gets ready to play. Rhythmic interpretation is free, emphasis on playing all the syllables of the dialogue and making the instrument "speak."

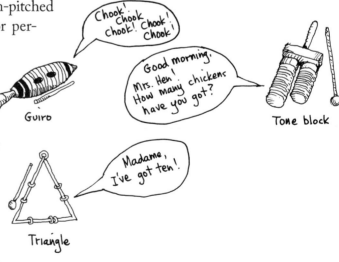

Adding Up to 10

Game: Quick reaction math. Keep a steady beat underneath. Change the numbers of yellow and brown chicks...how many speckled-red chicks does it take to add up to ten?

Variations
- If it gets too easy, pick up the tempo!
- Have students become the teacher in this activity.
- Students in groups of three. Third player needs to make it add up to ten:

Player one: "two of them are yellow" Player two:" two of them are brown" Player three: "six of them are speckled red" All: "The finest in the town!" (repeat at faster tempo until mistakes and laughter!)

Clap-passing game in the circle
Students seated in a circle, hands palms up on their knees. Right hand rests on R neighbor's hand. Beat is passed by swinging right hand over and clapping L neighbor's hand. The hand that was clapped swings over and claps next hand, and so on.

Sing the whole song (see score) and pass the clap in the circle on the steady beat. The person whose hand is clapped at the end of the song (on the last word, "town") is eliminated from the circle. Play until two people are left (these could become the two improvisors in the arrangement). Playing this game gets the melody of the song into the students' ears, and also reinforces the steady beat.

  Once eliminated from the circle, here are some things you can have students do:
- Accompany the singing with percussion instrument- don't forget to end with song!
- Get soprano recorders. Practice articulating the first half of the song on the note "G". Then on "A". Then on "C" and then on

"E" See if you can figure out how to play "Good morning, Mrs. Hen" using these four notes…

- Go to barred instruments and accompany with a light touch on octave Gs. See if you can start figuring out how to play "Four of them are yellow, etc." starting on high A…

Mrs. Hen in the Orff ensemble

A section: The challenge is going from the octave G accompaniment into the cascading "Four of them are yellow…"

Mallet Technique: Practice hand-over-hand technique on "Four of them are yellow" : R-L-R-L-R-L. Use patchen, snapping, then with mallets on the floor, on knees, etc. This is a nice mallet technique etude for the barred instruments. Slow it down so that the technique is fluid and correct! For young players this is virtuosic and fun!

Improvisation in two modes: Dividing the keyboard into zones can give kids a visual way into improvising over a shifting harmony.

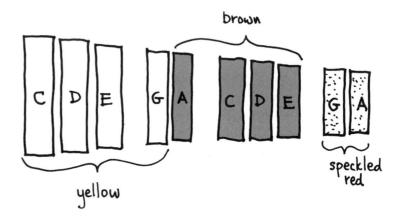

10 bars/Ten Chickens: You are Mrs. Hen, and as you look down at your pentatonic xylophone keyboard, you see….your 10 chickens! Give each group your loving attention! Touch and primp the yellow ones…. Play with the brown ones……tickle the two speckled reds!

Finding the borduns: Practice finding the border of each group. Play the two outside notes of yellow (C-G). brown (A-E) and speckled red (GA).

Game: Melodic range echo. Echo rhythms from body percussion where patschen is yellow, clap is brown, snap is speckled red….

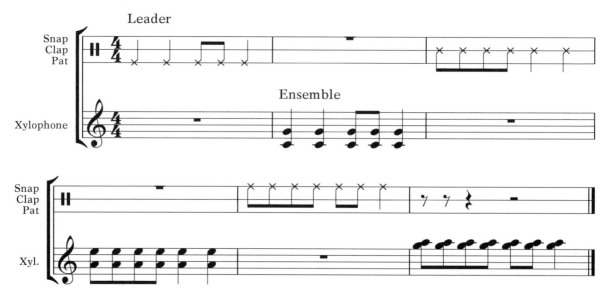

Improvisation B section:

Two soloists trade improvisation while the rest of the group (or just the basses) accompany on the drones. All join in unison on "Two of them are speckled red the finest in the town…"

Yellow One player improvises in the "Yellow" note set

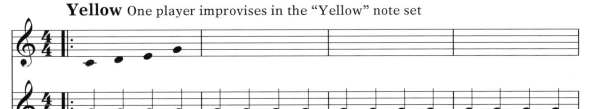

Brown One player improvises in the "Brown" note set

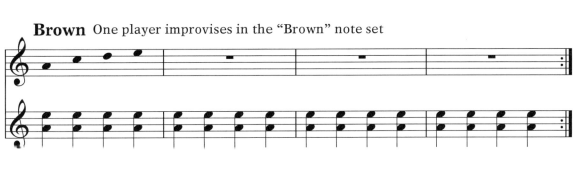

Speckled Red

Back to Section A

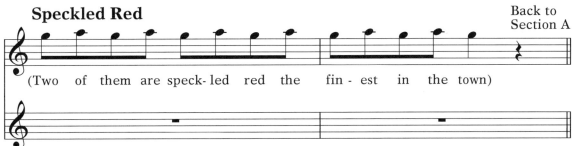

(Two of them are speck-led red the fin-est in the town)

two of them are speckled red

and four of them are brown

four of them are yellow

Mrs. Hen

Mother Goose

James Harding

Suggested form for performance

A section: Singing and/or recorders on melody, barred instruments accompany lightly on octave Gs

A section: Repeat

B section: Improvisation trade off….Yellow/Brown/Yellow/Brown... two of them are speckled red the finest in the town…

A section: Reprise

Coda: Phasing (see below). Phasing is the name for the shifting that occurs when several rhythms of different lengths repeat. Divide into five groups and try performing these patterns at the same time, where each group uses a different number of chooks. It's important to keep the same steady beat. Try fading out the resulting texture... Barred instruments accompany with steady, light, octave Gs while phasing is performed, either with voice or recorders or both. Fade out...

SHORT SONGS AND CANONS

SINGING FOR THE FUN OF IT

Singing Time at The San Francisco School
Every day at The San Francisco School 100 elementary kids from first through fifth grade come to the music room to sing with us for 20 minutes. This is not music class, it is something we call "Singing Time," and it arose out of the need to give the classroom teachers a longer lunch break. Singing time is sometimes an assembly, sometimes a chorus, and sometimes a campfire sing-a-long. Through the year, we sing hundreds of songs with the kids, from camp songs to folk songs to jazz standards.

Teaching short songs to lots of kids
We love Singing Time because it is the place where we can transmit lots of repertoire to our kids. It's also been a great place to hone presentation skills, since we need to engage the attention of many kids and get the songs into their ears and voices quickly.

Canons
Canons are perfect for large groups; only one melody is taught but the complexity that results from singing it in canon is very satisfying. Some ideas for teaching canons:

Make sure the song is strong before you try to sing it as a round
I often have each group sing the whole song before asking them to sing in canon with others.

Start with two parts, then add more
Make sure there are strong singers in each group! Have students lead sections when they are ready.

Encourage students to listen as they sing
It's not a musical experience to sing your part while blocking your ears against all the other voices!

Be clear about how many times each group will sing
If you will be repeating the song, practice the timing of the repetition with the group, and pay attention as a conductor to helping each group remember to perform the repeat.

Clarify the ending
If each group will end on their own, ask them to stay quiet and listen until the final group is done, then relax. Another option is to hook the canon, which means repeating the final phrase of the song until all groups are performing it together in unison. "Round the Oak Tree" and "You've Changed" are examples where hooking the canon makes sense. "The Spring Round" and "The Cuckoo Comes in April" are examples wherein each group ends on its own.

IN WISDOM'S LOVELY, PLEASANT WAYS

An adaptation of a Shaker hymn

Additional lyrics by
James Harding

Shaker Hymn
adapted by James Harding

In Wis-dom's love - ly, pleas-ant_ ways   I'll spend my days,   I'll spend my days   I'll spend my days   I'll spend my days   In Wis-dom's love - ly, pleas-ant ways

I'll walk with friends, both old and new
You'll learn from me, I'll learn from you
You'll learn from me, I'll learn from you
I'll walk with friends, both old and new

Though winter days will surely start
I'll keep the summer in my heart
I'll keep the summer in my heart
Though winter days will surely start

Shaker box

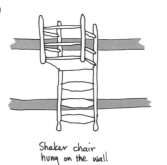

Shaker chair
hung on the wall

I found the original four-part hymn in John Langstaff's great collection: *Revels, A Garland of Song*. I adapted it to serve as a sweet anthem to start the school year.

Ideas for teaching
Use solfege to teach the answering phrase:

so do re mi do me re do

Practice singing all the lyrics to this melody. To prepare the ABBA form of the lyrics, you can play a game where you sing one line and the class sings back the companion line:

Teacher

I'll keep the sum -mer in my heart

Students

Though win-ter days will sure-ly start

Once the answering phrase is learned, start introducing the first and third phrases which you can sing solo at first, but soon the class should catch on.

The Shaker singing style is vigorous, not overly pretty. I like to make this a lively song, but I add a subito piano in at the line "Though winter days will surely start."

YOU'VE CHANGED!

A round that's also a game about noticing variation

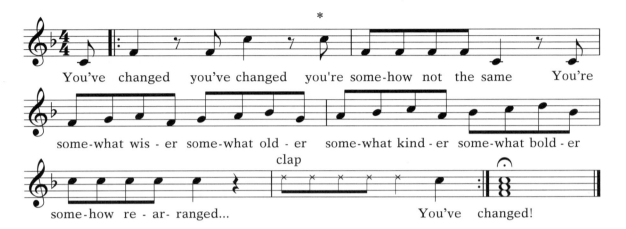

You've changed you've changed you're some-how not the same You're
some-what wis - er some-what old - er some-what kind - er some-what bold - er
clap
some-how re - ar- ranged... You've changed!

Game

This is a variation of a game called "Three Changes" which I learned from Viola Spolin's great collection *Theater Games for the Classroom.*[*] Drama games are all about attention and expression... so useful for the music classroom!

Set up

Students facing partners. If you are going to teach the song and have the lyrics written up, have students standing so one person has their back to the lyrics and the other is facing the lyrics.

Step one

Person with their back to the lyrics studies their partner carefully.

Step two

Person with their back to the lyrics turns to face the lyrics and sings song. Meanwhile, their partner changes something about their physical appearance.

Step three

When song is over, person who just sang the song turns back to their partner and tries to guess what changed.

Repeat game, switching roles and places

Teaching the Song

I like to teach this canon by first playing the game several times. While the students are focusing on the game, they are hearing me sing the song a few times, which prepares them to learn to sing it themselves later.

---

* Viola Spolin. *Theater Games for the Classroom* (Evanston: Northwestern University Press, 1986) p. 62

THE CUCKOO

A round featuring body percussion

James Harding

The cuc-koo comes in Ap-ril she sings her song in May In the mid-dle of June she

chang-es her tune   And then she flies a - way

Start with body percussion

The vigorous patschen figure is a good way of getting the attention of the group, and prepares them to sing the quicker words "middle of June she changes her tune."

(performed with alternating hands first on the right thigh, then on the left)

Add new body percussion patterns to the break

The second time you sing, add another two bars of body percussion rhythm. These could be made up by someone in the group.

The third time, add another two bars to the break, e.g.:

Try a phasing canon

If your group is up for the challenge, try performing the canon in three groups, where one group does the 2 bar break, another the 4 bar break, and the third the 6 bar break. Everyone starts together, but they won't end up that way—good luck figuring out how to end it!

Cuckoo!

A SPRING ROUND

This traditional song from Iceland is about the birds that signal spring. The
rhyme scheme lends itself to playful variation.

English words by
James Harding

Iceland *

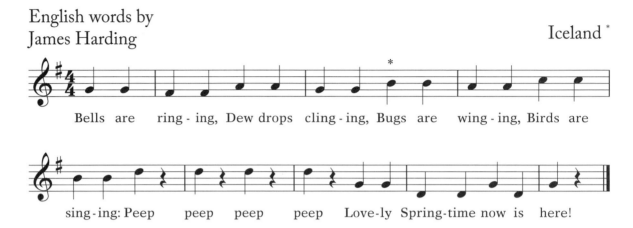

Bells are ring-ing, Dew drops cling-ing, Bugs are wing-ing, Birds are
sing-ing: Peep peep peep peep Love-ly Spring-time now is here!

Teach the melody with solfege

Before introducing the words, clarify the melody with solfege. This will help greatly to get the
very first interval in tune: Do Do Si Si Re Re Do Do etc.

Create motions for the actions

Ask the group for motions showing bells ringing, dew drops clinging, etc. Try performing in
canon with the motions.

Have singers create (and choreograph) their own verses

Invite students to create their own rhyming verses. Prime the pump by giving them lists of
rhyming verbs.

hatching	growing	soaring	peeping	zooming	warming	sprouting
patching	flowing	roaring	leaping	blooming	storming	scouting
matching	bowing	pouring	weeping	grooming	swarming	shouting
scratching	glowing	snoring	sleeping	booming	forming	doubting

Example: "Frogs are peeping, lambs are leaping, willows weeping, bears are sleeping! Baa
Baa Baa Baa Lovely springtime now is here!"

Since all the rhyming words are verbs, the verses will lend themselves to animating with
movement.

Frogs are peeping   Lambs are leaping   Willows weeping   Bears are sleeping

* I thank Kristín Valsdóttir for teaching me this round. Kristín is a founder of the Icelandic Orff Schulwerk Association.

Learn the original words in Icelandic

Original	Phonetic	Translation
Sá ég spóa	Sow yeeg spoa	I saw the spoa
suð'r í flóa	suth ree floa	Down by the bay
syngur lóa	ssyngur lóa	And the loa
út í móa	út ee móa	In the field
Bí, bí, bí, bí	Bee, bee, bee, bee	Bi bi bi bi
Vorið er komið víst á ný	Forth er komith víst ow nee	The spring is here again!

Spóa   Lóa

'ROUND THE OAK TREE

Great big oaks from little acorns grow. *

'Round the Oak Tree

James Harding

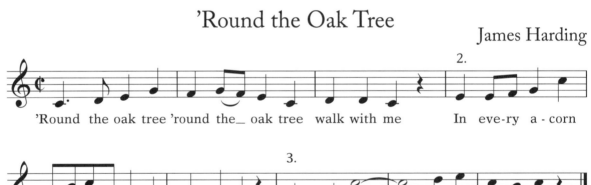

'Round the oak tree 'round the_ oak tree walk with me   In eve-ry a - corn

eve-ry lit-tle a-corn there's a tree   Some-thing great_   is in - side of me!

---

* I wrote this song for the dedication of a beautiful oak tree that was planted in the center of Marin Country Day School where I taught for three years. Holly Mannix, a wonderful teacher and administrator at the school used "'Round the Oak Tree" as the name of her weekly newsletter. I now dedicate this song to her memory. Thanks to Marianne O'Grady for the hand motions.

Teaching the song as a circle dance

I like to begin by singing while moving in the circle:

1st phrase: (to the right, stepping to the beat) R, L, R, L, R Close L

2nd phrase: (to the left) L, R, L, R, L Close R

3rd phrase: (face the center) stamp stamp on "Some-thing"

On "great" raise arms high with 'hitchhiker thumbs.'

Something great is inside of ME!

Slowly lower thumbs pointing to your chest on "me."

Once the group knows the dance and song well, we form three groups representing three important parts of the tree trunk.

The inside group is the heartwood, the support of the tree. A good place for people who know the song really well!

The second group is the xylem and phloem, the part of the tree most important to life. A good place for dynamic folks!

The third group forms a ring outside, the protective bark which keeps disease, weather and parasites from destroying the tree. It also makes the tree look good so it's a good place for your beautiful people!

Performance: heartwood group starts the canon, followed by the xylem/phloem and the outer bark. After two (or more) repetitions, the heartwood team repeats the last phrase three times until all three groups are singing "Something great is inside of me." The heartwood group can lead a gentle ralentando on the last unison phrase.

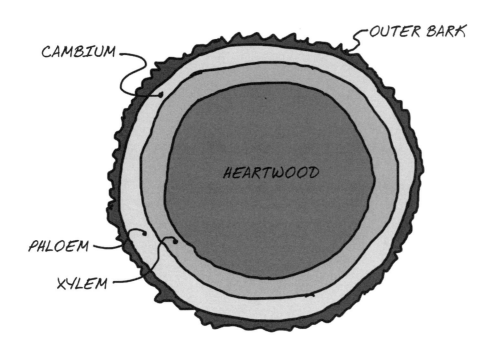

APPENDICES

Playing with the Elements of Music

Working With Musical Notation

What is Orff Schulwerk?

PLAYING WITH THE ELEMENTS OF MUSIC

Thinking like composers

Orff Schulwerk distinguishes itself from other approaches to music education in its emphasis on music as a creative discipline, where children make discoveries through active play with the elements of music. In this style of teaching, we want to inspire the children to think about the possibilities when encountering a new song or rhyme:

What would happen if we...sang it as a round? Played it on a different instrument? Played it twice as slowly? Divided it between two players? Wrote a different melody? Wrote our own words? Made up our own accompaniment? Exaggerated the dynamic?

In the pages that follow, I have defined six elements of music (Rhythm, Pitch, Timbre, Dynamic, Tempo and Form) and described ways to play with each. As examples, I've referred back to the activities in the book. My hope is that organizing these pedagogical ideas by element will emphasize that they can be applied to any poem, rhyme or material- not just the ones that I've presented in this book.

PLAYING WITH RHYTHM

"It is difficult to teach rhythm.
One must rather release it.
Rhythm is no abstract concept–
it is life itself!"

—Carl Orff (1895–1982) *

In the beginning, there was rhythm. The feeling for the common pulse is the most basic of musical perceptions, and it is crucial for playing music with others in an ensemble. You will notice that rhythmic speech is the starting point for many of the materials in this book, and that music-making featuring only rhythm is encouraged both as a starting point and as a satisfying end in itself.

How do we play with rhythm?

Building rhythms

Through language, manipulable objects and notation, we can invite children to build their own rhythmic patterns. You will find many examples in this book where children are invited to build rhythms from the names of things. In "Billy and Me" for example, children build ostinati with the names of tea utensils:

---

* Carl Orff *The Schulwerk:* Volume 3 of Documentation. (London: Schott, 1978) p. 17

cream
pitcher   sugar
               bowl

Exploring opposites and differences

We can vary rhythm to show the differences between swing rhythm and straight, and have children feel in movement the effect of varying meters. In "Loose Tooth" students march in 2/4 meter and then swing their arms in 3/4 meter.

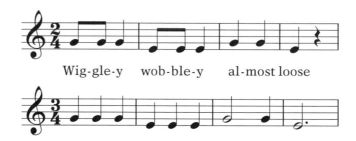

Wig-gle-y   wob-ble-y   al-most loose

Deciphering and translating

By going back and forth between rhythmic notation, rhythmic syllables and words that carry rhythm (like "chicken" and "egg"), we can playfully challenge students to translate rhythmic patterns across many systems:

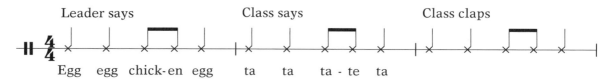

Leader says   Class says   Class claps

Egg   egg chick-en egg   ta   ta   ta - te   ta

Recombining rhythmic building bricks

This is a term used by Gunild Keetman in her book "Elementaria" to describe common rhythmic units of two- or three-beats. In this book there are many examples of activities featuring the set of two-beat rhythmic building bricks:

Creating rhythmic ostinati

These short, repeating patterns can be often used as an accompaniment to a melody or longer rhythmic phrase. In "Birds of a Feather," students make up ostinati from combining names of birds:

swan   woodpecker

golden eagle   humming bird

Layering ostinati

We can invite children to contribute their own patterns into a complex texture by layering several ostinati. Patterns can enter all at once, gradually in a pre-set order, or be brought in by a conductor. When layering ostinati, the most interesting textures result from variety in rhythm, timbre and phrase-length. From the lesson "Rules" here's an example of layering of three ostinati from school rules:

Noticing complementary rhythms

Two rhythms are complementary (that's with an e, like complete) when their patterns vary on all or most beats. In the example to the right, the rhythms are completely complementary (as well as very polite!). We can challenge students to create and identify complementary rhythmic patterns.

complimentary rhythms

Punctuating phrase structure

Since most of the materials in this book are based on texts, phrasing often links closely with the organization of the words. In some examples, all phrases are equal length. In many examples, phrases are of varied length. Noticing the rests at the ends of the phrase can become a musical attention game. In "Billy and Me," students explore the long and short phrases in a movement game:

Echoing rhythmic patterns

In echo exercises, we challenge children to imitate rhythms accurately. With experience, students can become leaders in this activity, coming up with their own patterns for others to imitate. In "Gregory Griggs" a student leader is echoed by the percussionists:

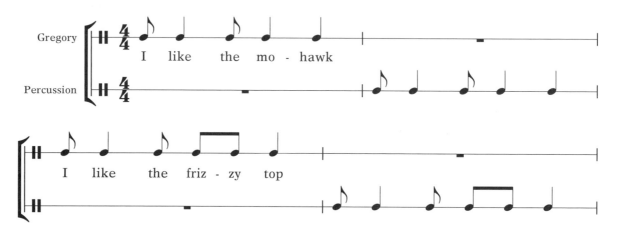

Perceiving and notating rhythms

We can use many forms of notation in rhythmic dictation excercises, where the challenge for the children is to hear the rhythm and be able to express it in some form of notation. One example of a form of dictation is found in "Mary, Mary, Quite Contrary" where students are challenged to express a rhythm in terms of plant names:

Improvising rhythmic answers

In this improvisational exercise the teacher performs a rhythmic question and the students improvise rhythmic answers. Usually, the answering phrase should match the length of the question phrase, but Orff and Keetman gave many examples of interesting variations of this exercise in Volume I of *Music for Children**. In the example below, the first answer differs completely from the question (but maintains phrase length). The second answer repeats the first half of the question and varies the ending. The third answer keeps the ending but varies the opening phrase.

Internalizing rhythms

When a child says a rhythm silently to herself, she is internalizing the rhythm. This exercise builds strong inner perception of the beat. In the lesson "The Wise Old Owl" the class is asked to internalize more and more of a rhythmic phrase until it is completely silent:

Couldn't we be more like that wise, old bird? ₹
Couldn't we be more like that wise, old ₹ ₹
Couldn't we be more like that wise ₹ ₹ ₹
Couldn't we be more like that ₹ ₹ ₹ ₹
Couldn't we be more ₹ ₹ ₹ ₹ ₹
Couldn't we be ₹ ₹ ₹ ₹ ₹ ₹
Couldn't ₹ ₹ ₹ ₹ ₹ ₹ ₹
₹ ₹ ₹ ₹ ₹ ₹ ₹ ₹

In the lesson "Boxes" students are asked to create a sixteen beat pattern including one rest. One variation involves internalizing the quarter and eighth notes and making a sound only on the one rest.

---

* Carl Orff and Gunild Keetman, Orff-Schulwerk: *Music for Children* Volume I (Margaret Murray Edition) (London: Schott & Co. Ltd, 1957) p. 64

PLAYING WITH PITCH

*"In order to compose, all you have to do is
remember a tune that no one else has thought of"*

—Robert Schumann (1810–1856)

Pitch refers to the frequency of vibration of a sound, something which can be measured and accurately described by units of Herz (cycles/second). Pitch in music is often seen as horizontal (the sequences of pitches which create melody) and vertical (the distances, relationships and tensions between two or more pitches at the same time, creating harmony).

How do we play with pitch?

Matching

Challenging children to imitate short melodic motifs is a way of building their pitch perception in the form of a game. Children can also take the lead in these kinds of exercises, making up their own challenges for their peers or for the teacher. In the lesson "Farmer, Farmer" individual students echo the teacher:

Exploring opposites

Pitch patterns can be used as signals for movement exploration (e.g. "move on tip toes when you hear the high notes, move close to the ground when you hear the low notes"). Pitch has many opposites to explore, including high and low, rising and falling, even forward and backward. In "Mary, Mary, Quite Contrary" students are challenged to sing melodic patterns backwards:

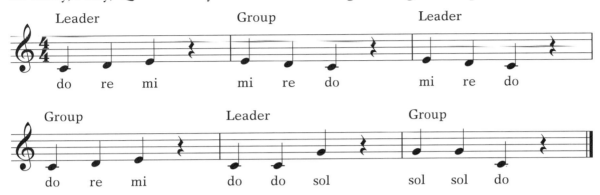

Playing in the pentatonic scale

The use of the pentatonic scale (in this book: Do, Re, Mi, So, La) supports the free play of children when improvising or composing their own melodies. The absence of half steps allows children to take rhythmic ideas and make them melodic without encountering the greater tensions and clashes of smaller intervals.

Improvising melodies

Question and answer exercises challenge children to create spontaneous melodic answers to a melodic question posed by the teacher. This is easiest at a barred instrument, where children can improvise without so much conscious planning of pitch production. This is more challenging vocally, and more challenging still singing with solfege syllables. Asking the children to start or end their improvisations on specific pitches adds to the demands of the exercise, and can be used to strengthen their perception of the home tone of the scale. In Gregory Griggs, children are invited to take a walk through the pentatonic neigborhood in question and answer form, with answering phrases ending on one of Gregory's "homes":

Composing melodies

Carl Orff said "Let the Children be their own composers." In this book, many of the lessons describe processes for supporting students to compose their own melodies. Flexible, visual systems where children can try out ideas by move pitches up and down can allow the class to compose melodies together. In "Betty Botter," ping pong balls in egg trays are used to compose a melody:

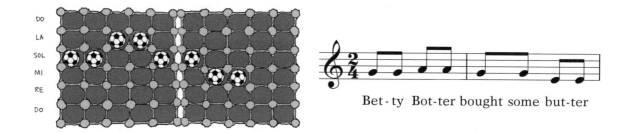

Bet - ty Bot - ter bought some but - ter

Crafting accompaniments

The use of the drone accompaniment in Orff Schulwerk allows children to contribute creatively to any arrangement. The parameters of drone accompaniments are easy to spell out (e.g. "Make up a pattern using C and G") and within these children can invent their own variations that then can be used to accompany melodies. In "Which Came First?" children make up rhythms with the words "chicken" and "egg" and then create drones to accompany the song. Some possible drones for the rhythm "egg egg chicken egg":

Varying notation systems

Switching between various systems of pitch notation, including solfege syllables, Curwin hand signs, grid notation, letter names, and conventional staff notation challenges students to recognize and decode melodies. In "Warm hands, warm" students enter the Curwin hand signs through touch:

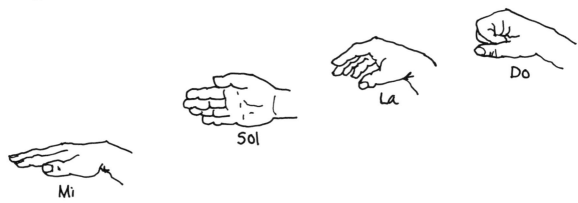

Games of melodic perception

Melodic dictation exercises challenge students to perceive melodic patterns and express them in a form of notation. In "Snakes and Ladders," students use pieces on a game board to notate melodies:

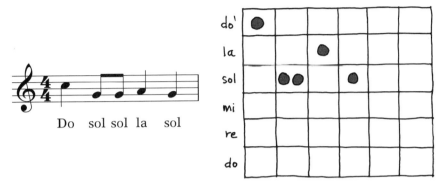

Do sol sol la sol

In "From Wibbleton to Wobbleton," students use two strings to show the relationship between a melody and a drone:

PLAYING WITH TIMBRE

"An orchestra is like a treasure chest" *

—James Levine, conductor (b. 1943)

Timbre is a French word meaning "sound color." Scientifically, the specific, recognizable sound of a particular instrument or human voice is a complex fingerprint of combined pitches called fundamental tones and overtones. Amazingly, the human ear and brain can identify these bundles as unique and remember their particular combination as "flute" or "mom's voice" or "Ella Fitzgerald," just as we can discern the many different hues of the visual color spectrum.

How do we play with timbre?

Recognizing timbres

Close your eyes and listen... Challenging children to guess what instrument is playing or which classmate is singing builds their vocabulary and aural perception. An example of a timbre guessing game is found in "Boxes," where students try to guess which instrument or instruments are playing behind the wall:

---

* Interview with James Levine, "Staying Power," *The Guardian.* 17 November 2000.

Orchestrating

From the moment we clap the rhythm of a familiar rhyme we are orchestrating. If we can clap the rhythm, we can pat it, stamp it, snap it, play it on a drum, cymbal, guiro or maraca. The diagram below shows some orchestration possibilities starting from the voice of the child and moving out.

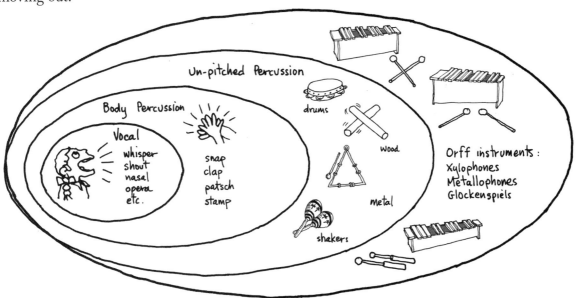

Some examples of orchestrating a familiar children's rhyme

"Lady bug, lady bug
Fly away home..."

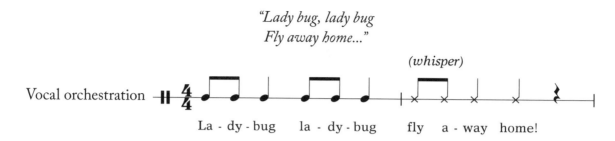

Body percussion orchestration (performed by one person)

Un-pitched percussion orchestration (performed by three players):

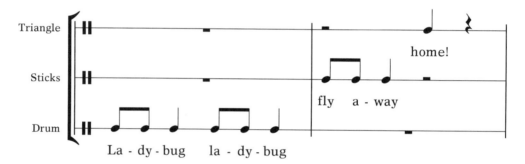

Exploring and inventing sounds

We can harness children's natural inventiveness by asking them to find their own sounds. In "Rules" students are challenged to orchestrate their ostinati with sounds made from objects at their desks. When invited to explore, children can find wonderful new ways to make sound with any percussion instrument, and can learn lots about the techniques of sound production in the process.

Scoring with visual symbols

We can use colors and visual symbols to represent various timbres in a musical score. "Betty Botter" shows the use of various decorated ping-pong balls to represent different timbres in a score made by an egg carton: *

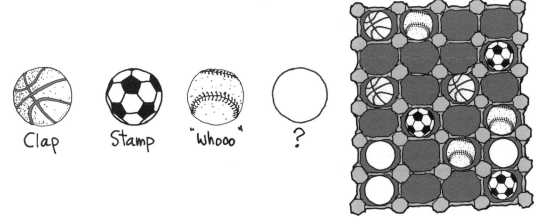

Categorizing timbres

Small percussion instruments can be categorized and sorted according to many criteria: shape (triangle, rectangle, cylinder, cone), material (wood, metal, plastic), and technique of sound production (striking, shaking, scraping).

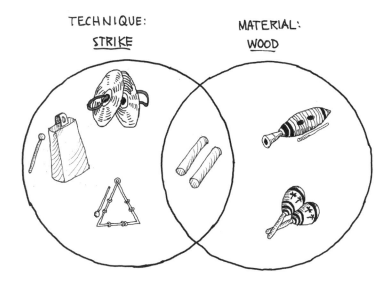

Dividing into timbre teams

Dividing the class into timbre teams can be useful for all sorts of exercises. Drum players move to the beat while stick players play the rhythm. Metal instruments play the A section and wood players play the B section. Have children help to make decisions about which team plays when.

---

* Ideas using ping pong balls and egg cartons courtesy of Onol Ferré. Barcelona, Spain (see "Betty Botter")

PLAYING WITH DYNAMIC

"At last a fortissimo!"

—Gustav Mahler (1860–1911) *

Dynamic is one of the keys to dramatic expression in music, from whisper to murmur to brash fanfare and all shades in-between. I have often found that paying attention to dynamic can transform a young ensemble's playing from mundane to magical. Dynamic is also a parameter of movement, and creative movement and conducting exercises lead children to a much larger expressive pallet when making music.

How do we play with Dynamic?

Exploring opposites

There are many opposites in dynamic to explore: soft to loud, growing louder and growing softer. Dynamics can be signals for movement exploration (e.g. large steps in response to forte and small steps in response to piano).

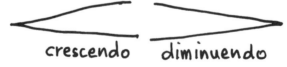

crescendo   diminuendo

Challenging children to produce the opposite dynamic in response to the teacher can be a fun game, as in "Mary Mary Quite Contrary"

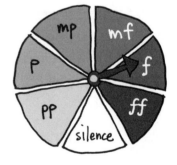

---

* Mahler supposedly visited Niagra Falls and was unimpressed. After conducting Beethoven's Symphony No. 3 a few days later, he stepped off the podium and said *"Endlich ein fortissimo!"*
Alex Ross. "The Niagra Fortissimo." *The Rest is Noise.* (New York: Farrar, Straus, and Giroux, 2006)

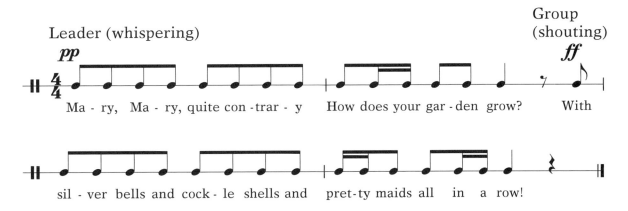

Leader (whispering)
pp

Ma - ry, Ma - ry, quite con -trar - y   How does your gar - den grow?   With

Group
(shouting)
ff

sil - ver bells and cock - le shells and   pret-ty maids all   in   a   row!

Conducting loud and soft

When working with layered ostinato textures, have student conductors play with creating crescendi and dimuendi, or sudden loud and soft. Conducting gestures can be worked out by the students.

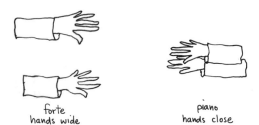

forte
hands wide

piano
hands close

Acting out the drama of dynamic

Young children in this culture tend to go loud by default, so we are often looking for ways to remind them of the beauties of softness and silence! Sometimes a dramatic image can be helpful in inspiring attention to dynamics. In the example "Billy and Me" the politeness of an English tea party calls for a light touch:

p politely

would you   be   so   kind   as   to   pass   the   cream?

PLAYING WITH TEMPO

*"I abhor the metronome, for I feel
that my blood and a machine
cannot relate."*

—Johannes Brahms (1833–1897)

Tempo is the speed of the music, telling us if the steady beat is slow and majestic or fast and furious. While for most ensembles of young musicians, keeping a steady tempo is our first goal, there are delights and challenges posed by changing tempos, both for practice and performance purposes. Establishing a clear tempo through effective conducting is a great exercise for young musicians.

How do we play with tempo?

Exploring opposites

Just as with dynamic, tempo has opposites to explore with children, such as fast/slow, and accelerando/ralentando. Tempo qualities are best experienced through movement. "Billy and Me" features an introduction where children act as water molecules in a heating tea-kettle, accelerating from stillness to a rapid boil, accompanied by friends at the barred instruments.

Moving to the beat

Expressing the steady beat to music over tempo changes is a great challenge for children. One example is found in "Boxes," where children are asked to keep the beat of a work song on the boxes while the singer varies the tempo:

Going twice as fast and twice as slow

Since beats have precise time values, it is possible to play or sing music exactly twice as slow or twice as fast. This is especially fun to explore in movement, and one example of such a game is found in the play-party "A Stitch in Time," where one dancer follows and copies another dancers moves but twice as slowly...

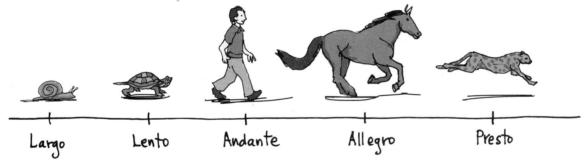

PLAYING WITH FORM

"Architecture is frozen music."

—J. W. von Goethe (1749–1832)

"Is music melted architecture?" *

—Jacques Barzun (1907–2012)

Form in music refers to the larger patterns which make up a piece of music. Form has to do with repetition and variation- whether something happens again, how many times, and whether something is completely new to the ear. In Orff Schulwerk, most of the forms that we work with are relatively simple.

How do we play with form?

Rearranging form

Identifying the various sections of a piece of music or the phrases that make up a melody or poem, we can invite children to vary their order and repetition. If we use visual symbols or objects to represent each part, children can rearrange them into new sequences. In "Snakes and Ladders" each symbol represents a melodic motif, and they are rearranged to form various melodies:

_____

* Jacques Barzun "A little matter of sense," *New York Times.* June 21, 1987

Creating and sharing in a rondo form

The rondo form (ABACADA etc.) consists of a repeating theme (A) that occurs between varied episodes (B C, D, etc.). This is a very useful musical structure to tie together many samples of student creativity. In "Loose Tooth," the Orff instrument arrangement is used in a rondo where the episodes are student skits about tooth traditions from many parts of the world.

Inventing variations following a form

Traditional dance music is a great source of clear musical forms which can inspire student choreography. Texts with repeating words can provide a form of repetition which can be used as a structure for student variations. An example is "Which Came First?" where students are asked to come up with their own gestures for the words "egg" and "chicken" which appear throughout the poem.

Building performance forms

I often invite the class to help think about the final performance form for a piece. We think about repetition, orchestration, and how to or if to include exploratory exercises or improvisation in the final form. I'm often drawing diagrams on the board, linking the various sections with arrows:

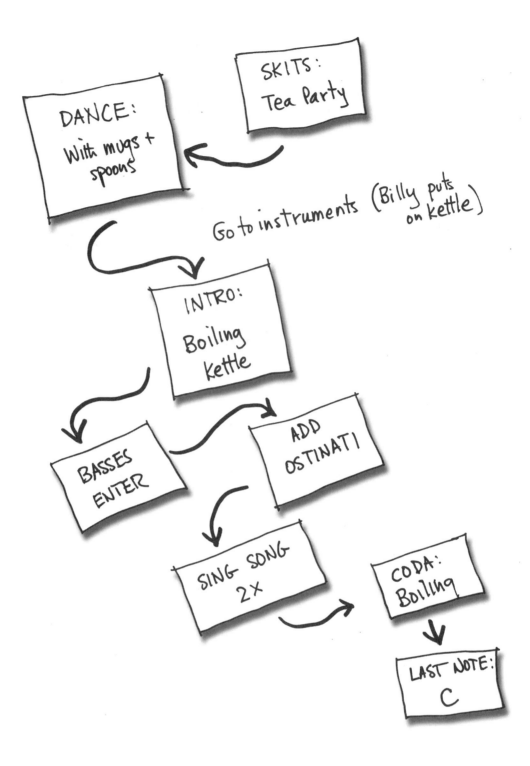

WORKING WITH MUSICAL NOTATION

This book explores many systems of musical notation, employed for the purposes of creating, conveying, understanding, remembering and enjoying music.

Why teach western notation?

Western musical notation is a very important invention, and can be credited with enabling the composition and preservation of a huge body of wonderful music. Learning to read music gives a person special access to these treasures as a performer and participant, and it makes sense that all humans should acquire this skill.

The cart before the horse

Many musical educators have placed so much emphasis on musical literacy that teaching music is now associated in people's minds with teaching the treble clef, quarter-notes and eighth-notes. Orff Schulwerk focuses on bringing children into the experience of making, enjoying and creating music, with conceptual understanding the natural result of these activities. If our musical time with children is limited, as it is in so many schools, I think our priority should be actual musical experience over conceptual learning, and all the more so, the younger the child.

Why explore non-standard forms of notation?

There are many ways of representing sound patterns with visual means (even tactile, kinesthetic and olfactory means), and this book explores some of them. I believe that arriving at musical information through many forms of representation reinforces the concepts for the students. The section "Lessons Featuring Props" contains a variety of ideas of how to use visual and tactile materials to represent musical ideas.

Incorporating literacy training into creative lessons

We need to remember that at the time of the development of the Schulwerk, musical notation and literacy was routinely taught in all German elementary schools by the classroom teacher as part of the curriculum. Since this is not the case in most of our schools today, many Orff Schulwerk adaptors have sought ways to incorporate more musical literacy teaching and drill into their lessons. There are examples in this book of such activity, and every lesson in this book could become an occasion for the review and reinforcement of music reading skills.

Rhythmic Notation

Stick notation

This is a simplified rhythmic notation without noteheads that makes it easier for young students to write notated patterns.

French time-name system

It is very useful to employ a spoken rhythmic notation system. Many cultures convey rhythm through special syllables, most famously Indian classical music. The French time name system has an advantage over the ta titi syllables in that there is no ambiguity about the exact location of each subdivision (see examples 4 and 5 below). * Of course, any rhythmic syllable system can be used to teach the examples in this book.

Rhythmic building bricks

As discussed in the pages on "Playing with Rhythm," Gunild Keetman proposed making young children familiar with five basic rhythmic building bricks:

There are many examples in this book where these bricks are represented by objects. The objects can then be used as rhythmic notation symbols for the purposes of composing rhythmic ostinati. Choosing a category and sorting words which match these rhythms is another approach, exemplified in "Birds of a Feather."

swan
duck
goose
crow
owl

ra-ven
sea-gull
pigeon.
spoonbill

woodpecker
kingfisher
flycatcher

hummingbird
parakeet
mynah bird

golden eagle
redwingblackbird
snowy egret

Another approach to combining two-beat rhythmic blocks is found in "How Many Miles to Babylon?" where students create ostinati in 6/8 meter by combining rhythms that represent the four points of the compass:

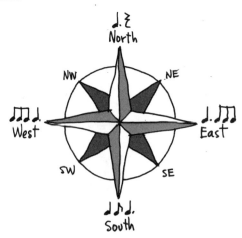

---

* The French time names were developed by Aime Paris in the 19th century. See Doug Goodkin's article "Rhythmic Vocalization" in *Play, Sing & Dance* (London: Schott, 2002) p. 129

Bigger bricks

Cards showing four beat and three beat and five beat patterns become useful for work with more experienced students, as well as cards showing more complex rhythms and compound meters like 6/8. These cards can be used for drill and review and also be incorporated into other lessons. In "Diddle Diddle Dumpling" four-beat rhythms on cards are tucked into slippers and passed around the circle:

Pitch notation

Solfege

This book uses a moveable solfege, which is the standard system for pitch syllables in both Orff and Kodaly. This means that the syllables Do,Re,Mi,Fa,Sol, La, and Ti are not matched with any absolute pitch, but can be used to show relationships of pitches in the scale. In other words, Sol-mi can be G-E when the song is in C, but Sol-Mi can be A-F# when a song is in D major. One advantage for using moveable solfege in combination with the Orff instruments is that the visual pattern of the instruments reinforces the solfege. Setting up an instrument in F pentatonic, children can see that the three bars in a row, (Do, Re, Mi) are now F, G and A.

Curwen-Glover hand signs

This is a very useful kinesthetic and visual notation which can support the use of solfege. With practice, students can recognize pitch patterns from hand signs and begin to hear intervals from sight. More information about Curwen-Glover Hand signs can be found in the Kodaly literature.

Other forms of notation

Box or grid notation

This system has been used by ethnomusicologists to describe music outside of Western concepts of meter. Each box is an equivalent sub-division, and the interaction of several rhythms can be shown using this grid:

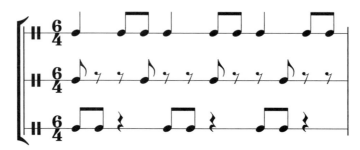

This would be the equivalent of:

Box notation can be represented with many materials such as egg-cartons, graph-paper, grids on the floor, and three-dimensional boxes.

Grids can also be used to represent pitch levels. In "The Crooked Man" a grid is used to compose a melody for the rhyme:

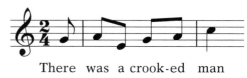

Graphic notation

Graphic symbols can be invented by the students and then used to create visual scores. An example of the use of graphic notation using yarn can be found in "Warm Hands, Warm," where children create a visual score made up of hand-prints:

In this kind of notation, children in the class decide how they want to interpret the symbols that they have created. Individual students can freely follow such visual scores as they wish, or a conductor can point to various patterns while the ensemble interprets them together.

For many other inspired examples of graphic notation, see Sofia Lopez-Ibor's book *Blue is the Sea* (Pentatonic Press, 2011)

WHAT IS ORFF SCHULWERK?

The activities in this book are all inspired by Orff Schulwerk, which is a philosophy of music and movement education developed by the composer, Carl Orff and his collaborator, the composer and educator Gunild Keetman. Here are some important principles of Orff Schulwerk that you will recognize in the approach of this book:

Making music is a natural activity of all human beings. Carl Orff said "It is difficult to teach rhythm...one must rather release it." [*] Going further, we could say that the main skills that are important to musicians, the perception of rhythm, awareness of timbre and pitch, and sensitivity to subtle shades of feeling, are all present in the normal activities of childhood.

Musical education of children should build from the child's experience. Orff recommended that we start making music with the materials and activities most accessible to children. Playground chants, nursery rhymes, spells, charms, proverbs, and riddles carry with them inherent rhythm and thus can be wonderful doorways into music making with children.

Teaching music means teaching dance, poetry, drama and sometimes math and science, too. Orff said, "Elemental music is never music alone, but forms a unity with movement, dance and speech..." [*]

Music is a social activity. Orff Schulwerk lessons make use of the collective attention, energy and creativity of the group.

Music should be understood by children. Students should understand the music they play and be able to use their understanding to improvise and compose their own music.

Music should be taught as a creative discipline. Carl Orff said "Let the children be their own composers." [*] Inviting children to create, improvise, compose and choreograph with the elements of music and movement is an essential hallmark of Orff Schulwerk.

HOW CAN I GET MORE INFORMATION AND TRAINING IN ORFF SCHULWERK?

Published resources about Orff Schulwerk in English

Besides the English adaptation of *Music for Children* by Margaret Murray, the North American adaption by Doreen Hall, and the American Edition by various authors, edited by Herman Regner of the Orff Institute, there are many supplemental publications about Orff Schulwerk in the English language. Orff's memoire *The Schulwerk*, also translated by Margaret Murray, is a wonderful glimpse into the mind of Orff, the educator. Gunild Keetman's practical volume *Elementaria* puts forth some of her pedagogical ideas, the first half concerning working with music and the second half working with movement. Wilhelm Keller, an early collaborator at the Orff Institute, published his own short and useful *Introduction to Orff Schulwerk*. In 2011, Schott published a collection of articles by the originators of this philosophy, bringing together compelling writing by Dorothee Gunther, Carl Orff, Gunild Keetman, Hermann Regner, and Barbara Haselbach about the aims of elemental music education. I have listed these resources and more in bibliographic form below:

- Goodkin, Doug. *Play Sing and Dance: An Introduction to Orff Schulwerk*. USA: Schott 2002

---

[*] Carl Orff. *The Schulwerk*

- Haselbach, Barbara. Dance Education: *Basic Principles and Models for Nursery and Primary Schools.* Schott 1979
- Keetman, Gunild (trans. M. Murray). *Elementaria.* Schott 1974
- Keller, Wilhelm. *Introduction to Orff Schulwerk:* Schott 1974
- Orff, Carl. *The Schulwerk* (Volume III of Documentation): Schott 1978
- Orff, Carl and Keetman, Gunild. Orff Schulwerk *Music for Children: Volumes I-V* (Margaret Murray Edition): Schott & Co. Ltd. London 1958
- Orff Forum Salzburg (Barbara Haselbach, ed.) *Texts on Theory and Practice of Orff Schulwerk: Basic Texts from the Years 1932–2010.* Schott 2011
- Regner, Hermann, Ed. *Music for Children: Orff-Schulwerk American Edition: Volumes 1, 2 and 3:* Schott 1993

Active learning for teachers

Although you can get many ideas through reading books like this one and the ones listed above, Orff Schulwerk is best learned through direct experience. A typical workshop or training class is a place of active learning, where adults are led into creative musical activity as participants just like children in the classroom. The understanding of an activity gained through participation is invaluable preparation for the teacher, allowing her to lead the children with the approach of a fellow explorer. In other words, don't just read this book: get out there and take an Orff class or workshop!

Some resources for further training in Orff Schulwerk

- The American Orff Schulwerk Association (AOSA): www.aosa.org
- The San Francisco International Orff Course: www.sforff.org
- The San Francisco School: www.sfschool.org
- The Orff Institute, Salzburg: www.orffinstitut.at
- The Orff Forum Salzburg: www.Orff Schulwerk-forum-salzburg.org/

ABOUT PENTATONIC PRESS

Pentatonic Press was formed by Doug Goodkin in 2004 with the following goals:
- To further the development of Orff Schulwerk through quality materials, ideas and processes grown from work with children of all ages.
- To attend to the roots of quality music education while exploring new territory.
- To provide a model of music and dance at the center of school curriculums, revealing their inherent connection with all subjects and their ability to cultivate community.
- To use music as a vehicle to reveal and cultivate each child's remarkable potential as an artist, citizen and compassionate human being.
- To offer full artistic control over the presentation of published material.

Pentatonic Press's growing catalogue includes six published books and two CDs.

- FROM WIBBLETON TO WOBBLETON: Adventures with the Elements of Music and Movement- James Harding: 2013
- ALL BLUES: Jazz for the Orff Ensemble-Doug Goodkin: 2011
- BLUE IS THE SEA: Music, Dance & Visual Arts-Sofía López-Ibor: 2011

- INTERY MINTERY: Nursery Rhymes for Body, Voice & Orff Ensemble-Doug Goodkin: 2008
- THE ABC's OF EDUCATION: A Primer for Schools to Come-Doug Goodkin: 2006
- NOW'S THE TIME: Teaching Jazz to All Ages-Doug Goodkin: 2004
- NOW'S THE TIME (Double CD): 2004
- GANDAYINA: West African Xylophone Music (CD)

Upcoming projects include such diverse subjects as guidelines for effective teaching, Ghanaian xylophone music, Ghanaian children's games, Indian music for children, jazz piano for all, intermediate jazz for Orff ensembles, pentatonic, modal and harmonic music from the world repertoire for children of all ages, a collection of songs for all occasions and more.

Those interested in having their project considered can contact Doug Goodkin through his website: www.douggoodkin.com

ABOUT THE AUTHOR

James Harding has taught music to children in the San Francisco Bay Area since 1990. Twenty years of that time he has taught at The San Francisco School, working with children ages 3 to 14, sharing the job with long-time colleagues Doug Goodkin and Sofía López-Ibor. Since 2001 he has been presenting workshops and trainings for music teachers locally, in the Bay Area, nationally for Orff chapters in many states, and internationally for Orff Schulwerk associations and schools in Canada, Brazil, Argentina, Colombia, Australia, Taiwan, Spain, Finland, Iceland, Estonia, and South Africa. James has been on the faculty of the San Francisco International Orff Course since 1996, and he has several times been a guest

Photo: Jes Smith

teacher at the Orff Institute in Salzburg, Austria. He has published several articles in the Orff Echo (AOSA quarterly) and the Orff Informazionen (magazine of the Orff Forum Salzburg). This is his first book.

ABOUT THE ILLUSTRATOR

Eli Noyes is an Academy Award® nominated animator who has done projects for Sesame Street, Scholastic, Nickelodeon, Pixar, and Disney. He is the president of San Francisco based Alligator Planet, an animation and graphics company specializing in education and the environment.